I0880250

PENGUIN ANANDA

IT'S OKAY

Jaya Sharma, popularly known as Jaya Kishori, is a well-known spiritual orator and motivational speaker. She began her spiritual journey in her childhood. Since then, she has given hundreds of discourses on sacred Hindu scriptures throughout the world. She believes that everything that has happened in her life was destined to happen. Her key interest and curiosity have always been in the spiritual plane; this has inspired her to immerse herself in it with fervent enthusiasm.

Her discourses are centred on the Shrimad Bhagavatam, Bhagavad Gita and the Ramayana, and she specializes in giving motivational talks on stress and relationship management, peer pressure, depression, parenting techniques, managing the generation gap and a host of topics for the searching mind.

Jaya Kishori is on a mission to help people become spiritual in their life. She believes spirituality is the solution to all our problems. She gives lessons on values and virtues that she believes are essential in shaping a beautiful life. The primary focus of her discourses is to restore faith and positivity among people who need confidence in themselves and happiness in the world around them. She tries to keep her discourses as logical and simple as possible so that they can be understood by all age groups, especially the youth, as they are the future of the country.

She has inspired countless people from all walks of life, in the path of righteousness and in living a life rich with the highest of values and ethics. She has been rewarded with numerous awards for her work, including the 'National Creator Award for Social Change' from our honourable Prime Minister Narendra Modi. She was awarded the Adarsh Yuva Adhyatmik Guru Puruskar (Ideal Young Spiritual Guru Award) during the Sixth Bharatiya Chhatra Sansad Award Ceremony in Pune, Maharashtra, in 2016; celebrated as Youth Spiritual Icon by *Fame India* magazine; and honoured with the 'Inspiring Woman' award by *Women's Era*. She also received the Most Inspiring Woman of the Year (Spiritual) at Global Excellence Awards (GEA) in May 2022.

She may be contacted at:

www.iamjayakishori.com
bookings@iamjayakishori.com

IT'S OKAY . . .

A Book *of* Inspirational *and* Mystic Thoughts

JAYA KISHORI

PENGUIN
ANANDA
An imprint of Penguin Random House

PENGUIN ANANDA

Penguin Ananda is an imprint of the Penguin Random House group of companies whose addresses can be found at global.penguinrandomhouse.com

Published by Penguin Random House India Pvt. Ltd
4th Floor, Capital Tower 1, MG Road,
Gurugram 122 002, Haryana, India

Penguin Random House India

First published in Penguin Ananda by Penguin Random House India 2025

Copyright © Jaya Kishori 2025

All rights reserved

10 9 8 7 6 5 4 3 2 1

The views and opinions expressed in this book are the author's own and the facts are as reported by her which have been verified to the extent possible, and the publishers are not in any way liable for the same.

Please note that no part of this book may be used or reproduced in any manner for the purpose of training artificial intelligence technologies or systems.

ISBN 9780143473213

Typeset in Sabon LT Pro by MAP Systems, Bengaluru, India
Printed at Replika Press Pvt. Ltd, India

This book is sold subject to the condition that it shall not, by way of trade or otherwise, be lent, resold, hired out or otherwise circulated without the publisher's prior consent in any form of binding or cover other than that in which it is published and without a similar condition including this condition being imposed on the subsequent purchaser.

www.penguin.co.in

MIX
Paper | Supporting responsible forestry
FSC™ C016779
FSC www.fsc.org

To the Late Mahesh Guruji, my nanu (maternal grandfather), whose love and inspiration have been pivotal in my journey. I know he is watching over us from wherever he is!

I MISS YOU!

Contents

1

It's Okay to Not Be Okay

The other day, I was at a get-together that was attended by a sizeable number of people. I could spot some known faces, a few were friends, others with whom I have worked in the past, all mingling among themselves, amid a sea of unknown faces. They were greeting each other rather warmly, asking one another about how they have been, how their life was going. Most were responding in a very similar manner and tone, that 'things were fine and that they were doing well'. Being in close proximity, I was able to overhear a few of these exchanges, when a question arose in my mind, 'Was it a fact that they were indeed doing fine?' 'Could it be possible that there be someone in the world with whom all things were good and fine in life?' 'And that nothing was wrong in their lives,' 'No work or task of theirs was undone'. 'That all or every of their relationships was good and none was troublesome or poor?' To me, it seemed impossible.

Then it occurred to me that they, quite like me, were following an old lesson we learn when still young. When we are often advised by our elders:

- **No matter what, you ought to be bold in the face of adversity;**
- **You must always smile, even though you are hurting inside;**
- **You must not feel too sad about anything;**
- **You cannot afford to lose in life;**
- **You cannot get tired so easily;**
- **No matter what's happening with you in your life, you must say, 'It's all okay.'** But the truth is, you are not!

In life, everything does not always go as we wish it to and to acknowledge this truth is our greatest strength. We tend to exaggerate and make a problem much bigger when we refuse to accept it. Life never runs perfectly; it is possible that on some days I don't feel okay; which I believe is perfectly okay. When will we realize that *It's okay to not be okay?*

It is not necessary to be strong all the time; like it is not essential to smile at all times. If you are faced with problems in life, you must bear with it—but it is important that you also remind yourself that 'things are not good' and that 'they are not running as you may have wanted'. Once this is done, you would perhaps be able to find a solution to the problem. If you keep feeding yourself with false beliefs about positivity that 'Everything is going fine' and that 'You really do not have any problem', then somewhere down the line, you are deceiving yourself. There is an increasing reliance and optimism that if you shoo away a problem or difficulty saying that nothing is wrong, or the problem or difficulty does not exist, you are relieved of it. This is one great fallacy. For the one in pain feels the pain, and no matter what is being said or needs to be believed, the pain does not subside on its own. This circumventing behaviour does not solve the problem. On the contrary, because you are not able to express the emotion, it becomes an added problem which is self-created.

The right way is to acknowledge that if you are in a given situation, then accept that you are in it. To be patient with that emotion is also a way to solve it. Remember, you are not the only one who is feeling this, there are numberless who are in the same boat—rather, most of humanity subsists in this. No one's life is perfect, no matter how perfect they depict their lives to be on social media, it is far from that. However, not everyone has the courage to accept this fact. Maybe, you could try to do that? Not for anyone else but yourself. To realize that real positivity is not in ignorance but in acknowledgement. It is not about ignoring or running away from a problem but in accepting it.

I know it is easy to say such things but difficult to implement them. I also know that if you are facing a difficult situation, you wish you could get out of it. I also know when a person is sad, he barely understands words of wisdom because of his pain and trauma. However, when one is in such a situation, one only needs to remind oneself that such a situation will not stay for long; it is only a passing phase. No situation stays permanently. The problem with which you were concerned or worried, say, five years ago, are you still worrying about those things? So quite like that, even the present ones would dissolve. Until then, we ought to learn to live with them. Therefore, it is important that we feel their presence and learn from them before they pass away.

At that time, you ought to keep reminding yourself, like morning follows night, your dark days will also end with a bright dawn. And if you wish to see that beautiful dawn, you must also experience the night. It is a matter of outlook; some enjoy the night and find it soothing; others are scared of it. So when you know that you need to pass the night, it makes a lot more sense that you pass it with a sense of tolerance and patience. Who knows, it might help to make your morning a little more beautiful than you had imagined. So it's okay to not feel okay, but not okay to suppress those emotions and act as if everything is okay.

Know the hard times shall soon pass
Though long and dark is your night;
Be patient and have some faith
A new dawn shall bring forth light.

2

It's Okay to Let Go

This happens to be the most difficult task in our lives but also the most important. Let us stop loving those who do not love us, or do not try to understand our emotions.

Sometimes in life, there are decisions which can change and completely turn our lives on their heads. One, and perhaps the most important of them, is choosing our partners. And if this goes wrong, then every other plan can go horribly wrong. Sometimes we can also make out that our decision has gone wrong, yet we do not try to end the relationship. Reason, we are paranoid that if the person we love is out of our life, would we find another? Would we be able to find happiness again? Can we start once again in a new relationship? And it is this fear that goads us to keep giving that person multiple chances. And this becomes our biggest mistake, a fatal blunder.

I am not saying you do not give your relationship a chance; also I am by no means stating that you do not make an effort to improve your relationship. But there comes a time when we can feel within that the relationship has gone cold and is at a dead-end, from where the road leads nowhere. Because the ones in it keep having different conversations every day, but the situation remains where it stood before, nothing changes. I know communication is key but only if the communication moves towards a direction that brings about a change. If that does not happen, it is better to stop there for good. The truth being, no matter how many chances you give to the one you care for, at most you may be able to change a habit or two, but not their core nature.

It must be understood that whatever you tolerate in your relationship will multiply at least five times in marriage. Hence, it may be a good habit to close your eyes and mull over what you are going through five times in order to assess the future.

The feeling that whatever is not good or right about our partners would change after marriage may be completely wrong. In fact, marriage gives a person a sense of security, which in turn makes them show their real colours. If you have the luck to see it before marriage, and you don't like what you see, run!

However, before you come to this conclusion or decision, you first need to know what you want. Or else you will remain so in every other relationship you enter. We make an effort to know others but not ourselves. We love another person but not ourselves. We make someone a priority in our life but not ourselves. It is high time we end this when we are faced with such a situation. Therefore, let us begin the journey of self-knowing so that we make better decisions. When we truly learn to love ourselves only then can we relate to others about our love and feelings.

Something you must remember—this step is important but difficult too—never imagine that after you have begun to give yourself priority, people will love you more. Or that people around you will laud you for your behaviour. It is possible that at that point of time, no one will even understand you. They might even blame you for being selfish and for ending the relationship. But it's okay. As long as you know what the truth is and what your fact is, you do not need validation from someone else. The day you are able to explain this to yourself, and you believe in it, it will hardly matter what others think about you.

Remember this, not everyone likes people who stand up for themselves. Many are intimidated by such personalities, whom they perceive to be strong.

The most important lesson that I have learnt from spirituality is that your energy is the most precious thing; do not spend it on people who do not deserve it. And do not worry about facts like:

- What will happen in the future?
- Will I find someone else?
- Will I manage to find the right person?

Just because you are traumatized that you may not find the right person, you must not suffer with the wrong person. Once you know that the company you have kept is not right for you, it is better to leave that space and make yourself understand that *it's okay to let go*. Not everything is meant to be forever, certain things are meant to be good lessons in life, so that you do not make the same mistakes again.

To let go and move ahead
May be hard and painful too;
Know life always moves forward
From it you must take some cue.

3

It's Okay If You Don't Know Something

Let me begin with a small story. There once lived some frogs in a small muddy pond at the edge of a forest. They would spend their days happily hopping in and out of the water, swimming around the hyacinth and mossy banks and feasting on insects and flies that abounded there.

One bright summer day, a stranger came by. It was an old sea turtle who was visiting a friend in the forest. While passing by the pond, the bemused old turtle paused and stared at the frogs jumping about the pond, croaking loudly and boasting about their habitat. Seeing the old turtle looking at them with strange curiosity, the oldest among the frogs inquired, 'I've never seen you before. Are you a traveller?'

The old turtle explained itself, to which the frog asked enthusiastically, 'And what do you think about this wonderful pond of ours? You see, it's the best pond in this forest and also the largest and the deepest stretch of water there ever was.'

At this the turtle laughed and remarked, 'Your pond is the size of a grain of sand in a sand dune, if compared to the waters where I come from.'

Hearing this, the frog ridiculed the old turtle. 'You are perhaps too old and senile to understand what is large. Nothing can be larger than our great pond. It's the most majestic pond in the world.'

The old turtle patiently explained, 'Look, my dear friend, you live in a water hole and have no idea of how large a sea can be. It's a hundred times larger than the forest that borders your little pond.'

Hearing their conversation, the other frogs joined in and looked at the old turtle disbelievingly. The turtle went on to say, 'The sea is so large that millions of frogs your size would be lost in it.'

'Nothing can ever be larger than our pond, you silly old fellow. Perhaps you are hallucinating,' rebuked the oldest among the pond-dwellers. The others too hollered at the old turtle.

Not showing any annoyance at the behaviour of the ignorant frogs, the old turtle asked them, 'How big do you think your pond is?'

To this, the oldest frog ordered his fellow frogs to show the turtle the measure of their pond. Soon, the frogs began hopping around the pond, jumping from one corner to another, leaping from one end to another, to display the size of their pond. 'Now can you see the hugeness of our waters?' The oldest frog remarked with pride.

'You will know what hugeness means when you get to see the sea I come from. The very sight and sounds of its waters will scare the daylight out of you. You will tremble with fear.'

'We showed you the proof and have no reason to believe you, for you have no proof of what you say,' said the oldest frog.

'Alright, then you come along with me, and I shall show you the sea,' said the old turtle.

At first, the frogs were unwilling and strongly disbelieving of the old turtle, saying that the old turtle had bad motives and would lead them to their death. An eagle-owl sitting on a nearby tree had overheard the argument. Wanting to conclude the debate, it advised that some frogs could go along with the old turtle and that they would be completely safe. The oldest frog, aware of the owl's wisdom, hesitatingly agreed. To which a few dozen frogs, and among them a very small and curious frog, decided to accompany the old turtle on a journey to the sea.

It was a long and arduous journey, and most were tired, filled with despair, and fell back on the way. Some were too frightened and felt they would never ever see their home again and returned. Each went back and gave the oldest frog their story—that it was a terrible lie and that the ones who were yet travelling would be deceived and might even be killed. Finally, when they reached the seashore after many gruelling days, only one frog—the smallest among them—remained with the old turtle.

The little frog trembled and shook with fear and shocked amazement, for he could see the blueness of the skies melting with the blueness of the vast endless sea. He exclaimed, 'You were so right, the sea is way larger than any of us can imagine. I wish my family and friends at the pond could witness this incredibly majestic sight.'

And the old turtle smiled and happily patted the little frog, content that he had proved his point and happy that truth had prevailed.

The story tells us the reason behind the behaviour of the frogs and why they refused to accept their own ignorance, thinking their own little world was the biggest and best. Often, we too lose out on things in our life simply because we refuse to accept that we 'actually do not know'. We feel whatever we do not know and are not aware of is either impossible or wrong. One should never go about projecting oneself as knowing everything. This is a strange ego that destroys a person's life.

How does it matter if you do not know about certain things and so are not aware of those? How does it matter if you do not know everything about the very work you do? And if you do not have enough information about things around you. Because it is absolutely okay to not know something, but it is definitely not okay if you are trying to discard some fact due to your own ignorance.

Remember, if you are not aware of something or cannot imagine it, it does not mean that it does not exist. It only points to a fact that we still need to learn many things in our life. Keep all the doors and windows of your mind open, for there is much in this world about which we do not know and we need to find out.

Only such people move ahead in life, who are aware that they do not know many things, and do not step back from trying to learn about those.

Everyone's life is like a little muddy pond, but in order to expand the horizons of the mind, they must first witness and experience the enormity of the sea. Only then will they be able to know and grow.

Ignorance is like a veil
Oft it tries to cover light;
Let knowledge dispel darkness
So that the future is bright.

4

It's Okay to Rest

We live in a world today where even if we were to work for twenty-four hours, a lot of work would remain to be done. Here, competition is running at such break-neck speed and time has become so crucial that resting can be construed as a crime. Sacrificing one's health and well-being to get work done is often glorified in society. Often, the ones who keep their balance and do things at a certain measured pace are bracketed as lazy.

A few days ago, I read something very interesting: people find many things important in their lives, until they fall sick. Only after falling sick do they realize that nothing is more important and sweeter than health. Strange that we always learn lessons after a bad experience. Haven't we heard from our childhood days: '*Pehla sukh nirogi kaya; dooja sukh pass mein maya*', which means that the first happiness is good health and the second is having money and resources. Going by this moral, even money takes a second place in life. Reason being that everything can only go well if our health is fine. Also, we can enjoy things only if we possess good health and cheer.

I am not in any way saying that you ought not to give due importance and attention to your goals and your career. You must work hard for your career but always keep in mind that you can only exert yourself when you are physically capable of doing so. It's advisable to not run too fast and stop; it would suffice to take a few good strides every day. This way, you keep moving towards your goal and your body gets the rest it needs. It is not an unknown fact that either you give your body a timely break, or else it will demand that break, mostly at times when it is most inconvenient for you.

Why is it that finding time for ourselves has come to mean a selfish act? It is totally okay to give yourself some rest. Or should I say, it is more than okay! I am aware that everyone is busy, they have much to do and have great responsibilities—I find people to be in such a hurry and rush that taking a break or some rest seems an impossible task. At the end of it, how much can you drain yourself? At the end, your batteries would get discharged and you would drop down in fatigue.

Remember, rest does not mean that you have taken a day off, but your mind is still into work. Nor does it mean that you spend your day thinking what all you would need to do in the next working day. This implies that your mind is in guilt about the day you have taken off.

You might even feel that taking a break might put you behind your peers in the career race. Before a lion attacks a prey, it always takes a couple of steps backwards. Do you know why? So that it can take a bigger leap. So if you need to take a longer leap in life, do step back before you exert yourself.

In conclusion, I would like to state what rest means. It means there will be some days of the month when you only breathe and relax or spend time taking deep, long breaths, admire the beauty around you, sleep endlessly, spend time like the little child you once used to be, without a thought for the past or for the future. Not having complaints about life. Taking life as if it were some game and always finding something good and interesting in things around you. Being exuberant all the time without reason; laughing and crying uncontrollably. And no matter what, as a child you had this intrinsic ability to find joy and happiness in every situation. When you manage to do this, you would have lived your life to a full measure. So it's totally okay to rest for a while, but not okay to exert yourself to an extent that you ruin your own health.

Running like an express train
Is like fast-forwarding life;
It will beget no pleasure
Except for traumas and strife.

5

It's Okay If People Misunderstand You

Buddha was once delivering a sermon in a little town where hoards had gathered to listen to him. Before ending he spoke a few enlightening words. 'Arise, it is time to wake up for your precious hours are passing by.' When his sermon was over, he retired to his dwellings. An hour later, he stepped out aware that a large number of people were patiently waiting to catch a glimpse of him. That being done, and having blessed them all, he went on his way.

While he was walking, he met a woman, who came running towards him and bowed down in utter reverence. Then she said, 'Oh Lord! I am a dancer and I had a performance scheduled, about which I had completely forgotten. But you are all-knowing, and when you spoke the ominous words, "Arise, it is time to wake up, for your precious hours are passing by . . ." I remembered my commitment. I cannot thank you enough.' Gently smiling, Buddha blessed her and continued on his way.

He had barely walked a little ahead when a man approached him. Having touched his feet, the man said with great reverence, 'I know you never judge anyone, so I must confess my truth to you. For months, I have been eyeing the home of a wealthy man, which I have been intending to break in and steal from. Today, I saw him along with his family attending your discourse, I also overhead him telling his wife that they were travelling to another town. Thereafter listening to your final words, "Arise, it is time to wake up, for your precious hours are passing by . . ." I knew you had given me the signal to proceed. I am sure I will succeed in my mission, and if I find a tidy sum of money, I will quit stealing forever.' Before Buddha could say anything, the man took to his heels.

As Buddha continued on his walk, the word spread that he was passing by and people poured out in large numbers to catch a glimpse of him. Seeing a large crowd following him, he decided to walk back to his dwellings. No sooner had he turned back, that a well-dressed old man, who seemed fairly affluent, came running towards him. Prostrating himself at his feet, the man said, 'Oh Lord! All my life I ran after materials things. Chasing money, gold, property, immoral things and other vices but your discourse today opened my eyes. Particularly, when you made the statement, "Arise, it is time to wake up, for your precious hours are passing by..." It felt as if those words were for me. I have now decided to shun a material life and work towards nirvana.' Buddha blessed the man and returned to his abode.

While he was resting, he could sense the acute discomfort of his disciples who had accompanied him on his walk and happened to witness all that had transpired. Understanding their predicament, he explained, 'Pay attention, my spiritual sons. I made the same statement to the entire congregation who came to meet me. However, it meant different things to different people. Each one interpreted it according to their own understanding, convenience and circumstances.'

In life, this is exactly how it happens. It is not necessary that a person takes your words in the same sense as you have meant them. Buddha had nowhere mentioned in his discourse that one should go for a dance performance or break into someone's home or work towards nirvana. He stated a simple sentence and the listeners worked on it as per their own conscience and convenience. Your responsibility is limited to the words you speak; it does not extend to the understanding of the listener or the mindset which determines the meaning they take at having heard the words. What the listener understands depicts their own comprehension, their knowledge and thinking.

If we take a closer look at ourselves, it would be relevant that when we have differences with someone, it is about the fact that our thoughts and feelings do not match with that of the other person. And we immediately go about trying to ensure that the person across us admits that we were right and they are wrong; remember, no matter how hard we try, this does not always happen. Each person is different in a sense that their thoughts, feelings, upbringing and attitude differ from another person's. It has been seen in many homes that despite quite a few things in common, the children of the family differ starkly from each other. Therefore, imagine what can be said of the world and the possibility that they comprehend your words in a manner you mean them to be. The earlier you let go of this desire to be understood fully and completely, the happier you will be.

If someone does not understand or follow you, do reflect upon it and tell yourself that the person is not in your shoes and hence is unable to understand. It may not be proper to blame such a person for not understanding you, and it is equally poor to blame your own words and thoughts. For, your words and thoughts are your own responsibility—and I remember reading these wise words long ago, stating which I would like to end this chapter: You must endeavour to be right in your own eyes, or else remember people will be people—for they manage to find faults even with God, so it's okay if they sometimes misunderstand you too.

You may be misunderstood
Some people may get you wrong;
Let them answer their conscience
You need to sing your own song.

6

It's Okay to Struggle

I heard this story as a child from my father. It goes like this. Once a man found the cocoon of a butterfly. He took it home to observe how it hatches. The next day, a tiny opening appeared in the cocoon. Curious and fascinated, he sat and watched the butterfly for several hours as it struggled to force its body through that little opening. A while later, it seemed to stop making any progress, for it appeared as if it had gotten as far as it could and could go no farther.

After waiting for a while, the man was concerned about the insect and decided to help it. He took a pair of scissors and nipped the remaining bit of the cocoon. Soon after, the butterfly emerged easily.

But alas, it could not unfurl its wings and fly gracefully. The butterfly had a swollen body and shrivelled wings. The man continued to watch the newborn butterfly, hoping that the wings would enlarge and expand to be able to support the body, which would contract in time.

Neither happened. In fact, the butterfly spent the rest of its life crawling around with a swollen body and deformed wings. The sad bit being that it was never able to fly.

What the man in his kindness and haste did not understand was that the small opening in the cocoon and the struggle were much needed for the butterfly to find its way through it. It was nature's way of forcing fluid from the body of the butterfly into its wings, so that it would be ready for flight once it achieved its freedom from the cocoon. His folly had cost the butterfly a healthy life.

Struggle is another name for life. Should anyone feel that he or she would get to surge ahead in life without struggle, it is a complete fallacy. For every step one takes, struggle is inevitable. Sometimes it is in our circumstances, at times in our relationships and often it is to do with work. Knowing that we need to face up to struggles, it is better we stand firm and face it—for wherever we may go, it will shadow our journey. Should you find the way ahead a little cumbersome and crooked, and fearing it you try to find a straighter path, remember that the way may appear straight and smooth, but there are bound to be treacherous bumpers to negotiate. So, it matters not how the road is, struggles will find their way into your life.

Often, it so happens, that we view this aspect of struggle in a very negative way. It can be compared to a bodybuilder who needs to work extremely hard to build his physique. When he begins the journey towards it, initially he suffers from many aches and pains; he also needs to watch his diet and lifestyle at every step, which may sound easy but is extremely difficult. Only after having adhered to it all does he end up with a remarkable physique. So it is his struggles that enable him to build and maintain a good body. In the same manner, wherever you find struggles and dare to face them, they will go a long way in making your life better, provided you take them in the right sense and spirit.

Overcoming mental turmoil enables you to become mentally strong. Overcoming emotional rigmarole helps you become emotionally stable. And overcoming physical ailments helps you gain physical strength and fitness. At the end of the day, every struggle is in its own way trying to make you stronger and more stable.

Therefore, it is recommended that you stop running away from your struggles. For the harder and tougher the struggles are, greater are the chances of success and the story that emerges from it would be magnificent.

The lessons your struggles can give you cannot be measured in terms of degrees or diplomas. Today's struggles will lay down tomorrow's personality—therefore learn from each one of them. A diamond is a piece of coal that never gave up. The next time you feel uncomfortable with the pressure in your life, remember: no pressure, no diamonds.

So, it's okay if you are struggling right now in your life, as it will definitely make you stronger and wiser, but it's not okay to run away from them thinking it will make your life easier, because it will not.

Life is but a great struggle
Learn to face it and endure;
It will spawn much joy and peace
Your success it will ensure.

7

It's Okay to Make Mistakes

Since our childhood days, we are a little scared about making mistakes. Our elders have often warned and scolded us saying, 'Please be careful when you are doing that,' or 'Make sure you do not make any mistakes.' Guardians were heard admonishing, 'Watch out child, if you go wrong, there will be a problem.' But is it humanly possible for a child to not err? Have our parents and elders never made mistakes in their life? Did they manage to lead a perfect life always? Now, if that is not the case, how on earth can they expect it from their children or youngsters that they would not make any? Such a mind-set results in children hiding things from their parents out of fear of being admonished.

Let me give you an example. A seven-year-old boy was to remain alone at home for a few hours while his mother went out for household shopping. Since it was the first time that she would be leaving the boy by himself, she fed him and explained at great length about the dos and don'ts while she was away. She specially warned about keeping away from the kitchen. The boy heard his mother patiently and agreed to do her bidding. An hour or so after his mother had left, the boy became restless. His extreme curiosity, more so about the kitchen, where his mother would spend a sizeable part of the day, attracted him. Even though he remembered her words about not going into the kitchen and pottering around lest he get hurt with something or the other, he went there.

Having entered the kitchen, he looked around and opened the fridge door. The frosty, smoky interiors made him feel nice and he let his face absorb the cold moistness coming from within. Then finding a glass-jug filled with orange juice, he felt thirsty, and wanting a cool drink he pulled it out with one hand. The jug was full and heavy, and he nearly dropped it. By a stroke of luck, he managed to hold on with both hands but ended spilling some of the juice on the kitchen floor.

Happy that he had managed the task, he searched for a tumbler to fill the juice like his mother would do. Finding one in the sink, he tried lifting it with one hand while holding on to the jug with the other, and then trying to pour the juice with one hand he spilled some more onto the floor. His hands were already slippery with the juice all over it, and as he tried pouring some more, the jug slipped out of his hands and fell to the floor, shattering into several pieces. The orange juice splattered all over the kitchen and made a small pool around the broken shards of glass. Shaken at the mess he had made, he dropped the tumbler out of sheer fright, which also broke on hitting the floor.

The little boy then ran into the living room, traumatized at the turn of events. He knew his mother would be annoyed at what he had done, so his mind ran round in circles for a possible explanation. An hour later, when his mother arrived, seeing her boy she instantly knew that he was up to some mischief. Upon discovering what he had done in the kitchen, she asked in a dismayed tone, 'Why did you go into the kitchen and open the fridge when I had told you not to do so?'

Scared and nervous, he replied innocently, 'I did nothing. I heard a loud noise in the kitchen and ran there to find the jug on the floor.'

His mother got irritated and said, 'So the jug of orange juice fell onto the floor on its own? And who do you think could have opened the fridge door to take it out?'

The boy replied without thinking, 'Mummy, could have been a ghost. Could even be the neighbour's cat which keeps sneaking in and out of the house.'

The lady smiled at her son's explanation. She drew him close and cupping his cheeks gently with both her palms said, 'My dear child, I know it happened because of you. But remember, we all make mistakes. But it is a poor idea to lie and not own up to it. Good children must speak the truth. Do you understand?' The boy nodded in agreement. Then she said, 'Now come on and help me clear the mess.' Finding his mother was not as angry as he had imagined, he got up and readily helped her to sort out the mess he had made.

Always remember, making mistakes is not a weakness but strength. They are only made by those who are either trying to do something or learn something. Those who are trying to learn something new in their life often slip up; this is natural as compared to those who try to do nothing new and never err. We can only learn from our own errors and follies; therefore, if we do not make any, then how we can learn if it was worth doing it in the first place?

What we learn from our elders are the experiences they have gathered from their own mistakes. But we need to learn from our own, as we get first-hand experience. Moreover, such mistakes are our own and not someone else's.

There goes a saying, 'Your mistakes and experiences are your greatest treasures—and such treasures are only gathered from your own and not from hearing what others did.' So, it's totally okay to make mistakes, but it's not at all okay to not accept it.

If a mistake has been made, then accepting it and paying for the same, both need to be done. The mother did not deal with the child harshly, on the contrary she explained it beautifully—if he had made the mess, then he ought to own up, and clearing it was his responsibility. And good learners are those who avoid repeating their follies over and over again.

So let us remember that we must not run away from our mistakes. We must own up, sort them out and move ahead in life. The fun is in making newer ones and learning from them. It is boring to lug the weight of a single error and carry it around for the rest of our lives.

Mistakes are very common
It is normal to make one;
It's best to admit follies
Which are made under the sun.

8

It's Okay to Be Forgotten

Once upon a time, there was a kingdom whose inhabitants believed in an ancient superstition: that anyone who became the king would have their name written on a mountain of gold in heaven.

A young man who lived there was intrigued by this belief and wanted nothing more than having his name engraved on the golden mountain. He endeavoured like a mad man so that he could become the king. He changed his ideals, his ways of thinking and even his own characteristics. He spent no time with his family or friends, strove like a lunatic and sacrificed all his happiness and worked with a single-minded zeal towards reaching the highest position in the land. Luck was with him and after many years of uphill relentless struggle, he managed to become the king.

Years later and upon his death, he found himself standing at the gates of heaven. He felt a strange elation that his lifelong dream was about to bear fruit. No sooner did he enter the precincts of heaven that he found the gatekeeper addressing him rather rudely, 'What are you seeking in here?'

He responded with a sense of pride and ego, 'What makes you speak to me in that tone? Are you not aware that I am a king?'

The gatekeeper scorned him. 'Oh! I've seen many kings like you come and go from here. It would be better if you do not waste my time and tell me the purpose of your visit.'

The king replied eagerly, 'I need to find the mountain of gold where I can etch my name.'

'Go straight ahead and turn to your right, there you will find what you are looking for,' said the gatekeeper rather indifferently.

The king went the way he was told and came upon the golden mountain. However, his elation turned to despair when he saw that every square inch of the mountain had some name or the other etched upon it, so much so that there was no space where he could write his own name. Dejected and disappointed, he returned to the gatekeeper and asked, 'There seems not a square inch of space on that mountain where I could possibly write anything. How then can I write my name on it?'

The gatekeeper gave him a sarcastic smile and said, 'Wipe out any name you wish and write your name there.'

The king stood perplexed and shocked at these words thinking to himself, 'Nothing could be stranger and more ridiculous, for if he could rub out someone's name and put his there, someday some other king would come and wipe out his.

We have not come to planet Earth to stay forever, we have all been given limited time to live our lives. Each one of us wishes and works in a fashion that after we are gone, we would be remembered for our work, name and fame and our notable attainments. In truth, even the greatest of kings on earth have been forgotten. Their name, fame and worldly achievements are barely remembered by anyone now. Quite like this, someday even your name and fame would be forgotten by people. If this be so, isn't it far better that you live your life in a manner that, when it is time to die, you feel deep contentment within that you have lived by your own principles and self-gotten values and not as per the whims, beliefs and dictates of society?

At this I happen to remember a few lines of a poem which used to be sung by the great saint Kabir:

ऐसा सख्त था महाराज,
जिनका मुल्कों में राज
जिन घर झूलता हाथी
ओ,
जिन घर झूलता हाथी,
रे,उन घर दिया ना बाती
झोंका पवन का लग जाए,
झपका पवन का लग जाए
काया धूल हो जासी,
काया तेरी धूल हो जासी
मत कर माया को अहंकार,
मत कर काया को अभिमान
काया गार से काची

So austere was the king
His kingdom spreading far and wide
Elephants would sway in his courtyards
Oh!
Those courtyards where elephants swayed
There's none to even light an oil lamp there
A gust of wind touched upon it all
A blast of wind blew upon it
And the body turned to dust
The body turned into dust
Don't let Maya get arrogant
Don't be proud of your body
The body is weaker than sand

It shouldn't be that in your rush and endeavour to accommodate yourselves within the parameters of society, you forget to live the most precious and memorable moments of your life. And should that happen, when you reach the other world, the gatekeeper standing there will tell you the exact words he had told the king.

Name and fame are sandcastles
Which are built on the seashore;
A single wave flattens it
Till someone else—makes one more.

9

It's Okay to Fear the Truth

We had a get-together of family and friends at home some time ago. Among those invited was a doctor, who is a good friend of my father's.

The invitees were talking among themselves about their life and problems. Quite a few were asking about their health and lifestyle issues, knowing that a doctor was at hand. At this, the doctor asked, 'What was the last time you had a complete body check-up?'

Some said six months ago, others mentioned that it had been a year, and so on and so forth.

One among them remarked that he never chanced a check-up. The doctor advised that it was wrong to not have a health check-up once past the fortieth year. He added that after attaining the age of forty, a couple of check-ups every year was advisable.

Here, the discussion heated up and the advice was debated upon.

I was standing nearby and listening. The man stated that he felt that health check-ups were a waste, as the reports would mention a million problems about sugar, cholesterol, thyroid and a host of various health issues, irrespective of whether they really existed or not. And the day he would go for one, he would deem himself sick, so it was better he never had one.

Having heard his statement, I wondered about the illusion people lived with, that if a person did not go for a health check-up, it would keep away diseases or sickness.

This incident taught me a lesson, if one does not face up to the truth, it surely doesn't mean that it will end on its own or disappear. My grandmother told me this when I was a child, 'When a cat drinks milk on the sly at someone's house, it keeps its eyes shut. Because it mistakenly feels that if it is not seeing anyone, then no one can see it.'

I am not sure about the truth behind this, but I do know that there is a strong lesson here. That closing your eyes to a situation will not end or finish it, but it gets a lot worse in the future, so much so that it becomes difficult to handle it.

Quite like what that person in the party, who felt that if he did not go for a test there would be no diagnosis, and therefore no reports on any disease. The man ignorantly felt that if a report is not made then how would any disease appear. He failed to appreciate that diseases do not happen on paper but in the body. He failed to realize that whether it is written or not, the disease, if present, will not vanish. Therefore, if there is some disease and it is treated in due time, perhaps a tube of ointment would cure it.

However, if left untreated, it would at a later date become very difficult to treat it. Also, if discovered later, it may have turned chronic and untreatable and would need a very painful remedy which would be difficult to tolerate. Here, you must understand that I am not just talking about a disease.

It is better to treat trouble or a situation when it is small or appears for the first time. It's far better that an ugly truth is faced and lessons learnt from it, so that we do not have to face it again. So, it's okay to be scared of the truth but not okay to not face it.

Truth is oft bitter and feared
Yet, it makes the world go round;
Know, lies make much hue and cry
But truth speaks without a sound.

10

It's Okay to Be Discomforted

Once there lived a venue (group) of vultures. They inhabited a dense forest and were a merry lot. One day, it so happened that they decided to change their placc of hunting to a remote island which was not too far from the forest. Having flown there, they found the island enchanting. The most astonishing part of it was that food was in abundance there. They did not even need to hunt for it. The situation made them extremely happy and content. Soon they all settled on that island and had quite forgotten about the jungle, which was their home.

A few months later, the older and wiser vultures felt that living on the island was making their lot incompetent and incapable of doing what they were good at. Their hunting skills were being badly compromised. They had grown used to a very comfortable and easy living. Experience had taught them that it was a dangerous situation. So, they gathered their younger ones and asked them to consider going back to the forest. Most of the younger lot argued against this idea. They were happy living on the island and did not think going back was a good option.

The older vultures tried hard to convince the rest, but their idea was strongly resisted. Unable to make the rest change their mind, a few of the oldest ones left the island, flew back to the jungle and returned to their previous lifestyle.

A few months passed by. The older ones concerned at how the rest were faring on the island went there to visit and were greeted by the most shocking sight. Most of their fellow vultures on the island lay dead. The few they found alive were in a tragic condition. They were about to die. When asked as to what had happened to them, one of the dying vultures related their tragic tale.

It narrated that leading an easy and comfortable life had made them all complacent. They had forgotten how to hunt and live like birds of prey. Their talons had lost their razor sharpness, and their beaks had become soft and brittle. One day, a boat came upon the island and some animals from the boat were set free there. Among them were leopards, wolves and hyenas. The animals took to eating whatever they could find on the island. The vultures and other birds living there made easy prey. Reason, they had forgotten the art of fighting, had grown physically unfit to defend themselves, and thus became soft targets for the marauding animals. Their piteous situation was the direct outcome of this.

It often happens in our life that we get so comfortable in our situation that the very thought of getting out of it terrifies us. We are scared to do something different, nervous about learning something new. We forget that, in life, things are not always meant to be right and effortless. When life flows smoothly, it is comforting and easy, but we must always remember that difficult times come too; and God forbid when they do, it will become impossible for us to handle them. Reason, we never made ourselves tough and worked on being smart enough to handle adverse situations.

No wonder successful people the world over teach us that one must learn some new task or skill, maybe a new language, or perhaps take up a new hobby. It is important that everyone must try to do something different than the mundane in life. It is a simple technique to come out of our comfort zones. Like with time, an axe needs to be sharpened; machines need to be kept in good working condition or else they get rusted. Quite like this, our minds and bodies must be put to newer challenges and tests, so that they remain active, alert and in good working order. So, when problems like wild leopards pounce upon us, we are capable of fighting and defeating them.

It's okay if we sometimes feel discomforted and challenged, but not okay if we are looking for an exit route out of every such trying situation which may befall us in life.

Life's a mix of myriad hues
It never comforts all through;
Hardships will befall us all
We must bear their burdens too.

11

It's Okay to Say No

We are often taught that those who obey their elders and listen to what others have to say, also ones who think about others before they think of themselves, are good people. But is this definition of 'goodness' a correct one? Is it true that those who always listen to others, obey others and try to make everyone else happy are good human beings? I don't think so. In my eyes, a good person is one who is understanding and wise. And a wise person knows when to say 'yes' and when to say 'no'. Whom do we need to listen to and whom do we need to ignore? The person who can decipher this difference is in essence a good and a wise person.

The very task of saying 'no' is a hard and a trying task for us. This compulsion to say 'yes' always, at times backfires and even harms us. But you must understand a simple fact: how often can we make the people around us happy? What happens is that by always sacrificing our inner peace for the sake of others, just because we need to say 'yes', results in a gross disturbance in our minds and hearts, which pours out from our beings someday in an ugly fashion.

I will share a personal experience with you. Due to my work and profession, it often happened that people would come to me with their problems and difficulties. Sometimes friends and family, and at times even unknown people have approached me. When I first began handling these situations, I began to feel very responsible for it all and for all those who came to me seeking some advice or suggestion. It would occur to me that how on earth could I tell someone a 'no' when they needed me? It was irrespective of the time and situation when they sought my help. I got into the habit of saying 'yes' to everyone who came to me, at all times in my willingness to be of use and help.

When they needed me desperately, I was there. When they wanted to rant about things, I was there. When they needed help I was there. When they wanted some advice I was there. I was always there. Time passed and I kept up with the task of always being there. But problems appear in everybody's life; everyone is fighting some battle of its kind and is worried about something or the other. No one's life is easy. We may even at times feel that someone else's life is a bed or roses, but in truth it is never so. Mine too was never an easy life. Yet, even in such times, I could never bring myself to say 'no'.

Then one day, the dam of my patience collapsed, and that made me react in a fashion I had never reacted before. I began venting out my anger at all and sundry, almost as if there was a volcanic explosion within and that was spewing fire at everyone around. I suddenly had a feeling: why was no one trying to understand *me* or *my* issues? But perhaps it was my folly of getting into this bad habit of always saying 'yes' to them, and addressing their problems in priority to my own, which had in a way spoilt their way of thinking. At this, the ones close to me embraced me and tried to hear me out. Among them, those who loved me understood my plight and quandary. But a few even complained that I had changed, and I was not like I used to be. And this was because I had learnt to say 'no' to people.

And on that very day, I got one of my biggest lessons in life. People will only like you and will keep liking you till the time you listen to them, be of use to them and give due regard to their feelings. It is strange and true that the day you start thinking about yourself, you are labelled selfish. A single instance of saying a 'no' submerged all my previous 'yeses'. That was the day I realized how important it was to say 'no'!

There should be nothing abnormal about a fact—when we are approached by someone for a problem they are facing, or that they wish to rant about a situation in their life, maybe even share some feeling they are caught up with and we reply—'no, not today'. The reason for saying so may be anything. Maybe, that day we are happy and do not wish that we spoil our mood. Could be that we ourselves are feeling low and down and do not wish to add someone else's issues to it. In such situation, we ought to learn to say a 'no'. It is not important, nor required to stand up for others' needs at all times.

Sometimes, thinking about our own needs and comforts is also good. We need to give up this zest of trying to be good and nice to others at all times and for a change try to be good to ourselves. So, it's totally okay to say 'no' and keep your mental peace and not okay to say 'yes' and ruin our inner happiness.

How hard it is to say 'no'
And harder to turn our face;
It's fine art we need to learn
Lest we bring ourselves disgrace.

12

It's Okay to Be on the Wrong Path

We are often confused about a number of things in our life; we even attempt to do newer things. This may relate to our work, at times it is our relationships, and sometimes it is our behaviour. However, while we are engrossed with what is ongoing, it is not always necessary that we know what is right and what is wrong. Yet, we move ahead with it because it often happens that we only find out what is right and wrong *after* we are done with whatever we are doing.

The problem is not about doing something new. The problem relates to the fact that sometimes the difficulty or problem is in front of our eyes, but we fail to address it. We ourselves indulge in self-damaging behaviour and realize later that it has spoilt many good years of our life. This could be our work, maybe a relationship or even a particular behaviour. We often take a long time to understand—where did we go wrong?

The issue stems from the fact that more often than not, the problem is understood by us, but we take too long to solve it. Because the truth is that when you are on the wrong path, often you are aware of it but prefer to live in denial. For example, if you are in a wrong or poor relationship, you comprehend soon enough that it will not last, yet you keep dragging it further, imagining it will improve with time.

You need to remember that sometimes things do not improve but get uglier with time. Just like if you are in a wrong job and realize that it will never bring you peace and satisfaction or that you will never be happy doing it, yet you continue in it. It is not surprising that each one of us has reasons to defend our point of view or attitude. Some say that they would never manage to get another job, others defend their decision saying that if they try a novel career it will backfire, leaving them with little choice but to pursue the old one. We state these feeble and flimsy excuses and keep suffering our circumstances, much to our great dismay and terrible dissatisfaction.

Most of us know what we need to do in a situation. When to start and when to stop and how to make changes, even though at times we pretend that we are not aware; deep down we know the truth. A wrong attitude is not doing the wrong things; a wrong attitude is when you know something is wrong and yet you keep doing it for reasons which are not tenable or that you build up as a defence mechanism.

You need to remember something: once you get to know you're on the wrong train, it is best to get down at the very next station. The reason being that the longer you continue with the journey, the more expensive the return ticket will be. So, it's okay to be on the wrong path, but when you get to know that you're going the wrong way, then it's not okay to pursue it further.

Nothing wrong in being wrong
It's a part of living life;
One must try to set it right
Keeps at bay much pain and strife.

13

It's Okay If Life Is Unfair

You must have heard the fable about the 'Fox and the Grapes'. According to Aesop, a hungry fox had tried to pick some bunches of grapes from a tree. He jumped a few times, failed miserably and left the place muttering, 'Oh! I'm tiring myself out for grapes that are too sour.' The ancient story ends here, packing a moral punch, referring to the popular tendency to dismiss and belittle something one cannot get. But I'm not too sure that it could actually happen with a creature as intelligent, as wily and as industrious as the fox.

In my version, the fox kept going near the tree every day and tried to get the grapes that hung just out of its reach. It so happened that on that very tree lived a raven that had laid fresh eggs in her nest. One day, she asked the adamant fox, 'Dear brother, though you're trying so hard, the grapes are too high for you to reach. Don't you get tired?'

The fox replied, 'I am trying hard and I'll try even harder. I'm sure finally I will have some luck.'

To this the raven offered, 'Alright, let us cut a deal. You see my nest is perched upon the upper branches of this tree where I have laid my eggs. A wild cat has its eyes on them. If you promise to keep that cat away from my eggs, I will pluck the grapes and give them every day while you stand guard here. Once my eggs are hatched and my little ones can fly, I shall depart from here and our deal would have been done.'

The fox found this quite appealing. It was barely much work to guard the eggs. Over the next few weeks, it kept up its vigil near the tree to ward off the wild cat. The raven kept its part of the deal and dropped bunches of grapes every day. The eggs hatched, and after a few weeks the raven with its new family flew away. This made the fox happy and content.

When life is unfair, try to be fair to someone else—it may be a fine remedy. Who knows it may bring what you desire the most, because you helped someone to fulfil theirs. The fable I just mentioned teaches us two lessons. First, the fox did not quit in an adverse situation. When we find such things in our lives which make us feel that life is not being fair with us, the first thought that comes to the mind is that we should quit. But this is the real test. For it is time you complement your hard work with some grit and courage. Success is achieved only by those who rise after falling, as everything depends on the courage to rise and not everyone has this quality. Failure is faced by almost every individual but not everyone has the courage to rise and move towards their goals thereafter. But you can be the one who does that. Because winners are not people who do not fail, but people who do not quit. On the other hand, when you feel life is not being fair to you, you could become so bitter that neither do you like someone else's happiness, nor do you want to make others happy. To suppress your own inferiority, you begin demeaning others, under the illusion that such acts will make you feel better. But the fox did not do this. He tried to make the raven happy and in helping the bird, got helped in return—something which fulfilled his desires too. This may sound bookish and sentimental—but if you have the intention of making someone's life better, it intrinsically implies that your life will be better too. This is the rule of the cosmos and exactly how karma works.

So, when you feel your life is not fair, you ought to try making it fair for someone else. Such a deed will result in a blessing. It is okay if your life is not fair but it's not okay to quit because of that; and it's definitely not okay that you make others life miserable because of the way you feel.

We often feel life's unfair
Know bad times come like seasons;
The cosmos plans everything
For its acts there are reasons.

14

It's Okay to Feel Anger

This is the story of a boy who habitually lost his temper and was quick to get angry for reasons best known to him. He would quarrel with kids in the neighbourhood and at times would lose his temper upon his friends and family. This habit of his made him unpopular and his friends and most neighbours ignored him. While his parents tried to explain his drawback in every possible manner, their efforts were in vain.

One day his father thought of an idea which he felt would help his son. He gave his son a huge bag of nails, and explained that whenever he lost his temper, he had to hammer a nail into the fence around the house.

The boy found this very funny but agreed to do his father's bidding. On the first day he drove some thirty nails into the fence. On the next day the number of nails he hammered was reduced to half. The boy found hammering the nails very difficult and decided to control his anger. As days passed, the number of nails he hammered kept reducing and soon came a day when he did not need to hammer any.

After some time, the boy told his father that it had been several days since he had hammered a nail into the fence. Then his father told him to begin removing a few nails every day. In a few days, he managed to remove almost all the nails save a few. The ones he could not were hammered very deep and could not be removed.

At this, his father asked, 'What do you see there?'

'Holes in the fence,' the boy replied.

His father said, 'The nails were like the bad words you hammered onto people. They left a scar on those people's minds. You removed almost all the nails, but the holes they left could not be covered up. The nails you could not remove are like the permanent scars on people's minds. They will remain there forever.'

Anger is not necessarily bad because it is an emotion. And emotions can become harmful if they are suppressed. Acknowledging every emotion can be a way to understand yourself properly. But when you react without understanding, you may end up making the biggest mistake of your life. When you are angry, you often do not realize what you are saying, why you are saying it or to whom you are saying it. Often, we fail to measure the effect of those words. When you are angry, you express your own emotions only and fail to consider the emotions the other person might have. It is not the correct thing to do. Remember, anger is an emotion that can last for a few minutes, but if it is not handled properly, it can destroy relationships of years in no time. Besides, it may cause wounds that can never be healed. So what can we do in such situations?

The first step: What you should do is stop talking right there and then. Get into the habit of telling people that when you are angry, you don't want to talk because you won't be able to take responsibility for the words spoken during moments of your anger. So the conversation can happen once you feel stable and are able to have a proper conversation.

The second step: When you are angry, do not take any decision. Whenever you get very angry, you feel as if everything is over or a feeling that you wish to end everything right there and then. The heart takes time to decide but emotions want the decisions instantly and we cannot run on the basis of such emotions. If we start acting on the pull of emotions, we may never be able to take a correct decision.

The last step: When you feel angry and you take some time off from others, have a conversation with yourself and ask yourself: what am I angry about? Is this really worth making me so angry? Is this emotion coming from somewhere else? If yes, then what is the reason behind this anger? Only if you reach the root of anger, will you be able to control it. Otherwise, you will always get worked up by something or the other and not understand the real cause behind so much anguish that builds up within. So go to the root cause and then work upon it.

Therefore, it is not wrong to have emotions, but it is wrong to fall prey to the illusion of emotions. You should not turn your anger into a certificate of being rude and disrespectful. If you have an issue, you need to resolve it yourself: no one can do it for you. Why should your dear ones suffer because of something you are unable to sort out or maybe do not wish to. Hence, if your emotions are threatening to spill out and harm someone else, your first step should be to correct and overcome them.

Finally, it's totally okay to feel angry, but it is not okay to be disrespectful and mean with others in order to overcome your anger, and just in case you think it might make you feel better.

Anger is a great spoiler
It can cause more harm than good,
To rein it in is an art
Not many have understood.

15

It's Okay If Your Plans Fail

It was 24 March 2020 when the prime minister of India announced a lockdown for twenty-one days. I distinctly remember that barely a month before this date I was sitting in my office with my team and we were discussing how we would plan our future work schedules. Every team-member was happy, the reason being there were three new projects in the offing during the year. To a measure we had planned quite a lot, the teams for the projects duly set up and the enthusiasm seemed unbridled. The year 2020 looked like it would be the best year of my life.

The meeting over, I went home and sat down with my parents to chat about the affairs we had discussed and about a piece of news that was doing the rounds—that a strange disease had made its appearance in the country. The disease it seemed was quite dangerous and there seemed stark possibilities that people might even need to stay home to avoid getting infected by it. Hearing it, a plethora of thoughts swept across my mind, as such a thing had never happened before. More so, how could people be locked up in their own houses? If people would not be able to leave their homes, how on earth would they be able to work? Moreover, how would they then run their homes? With such thoughts looming large in our mind, I went to bed.

The following two weeks we were busy with work and a lot more mundane affairs. I still remember, I was in the midst of a spiritual session in Cuttack; by then wearing masks had kind of become the mandate, fewer people were outdoors and other restrictions had begun. Even until then, I had little inkling that there could be a complete shut-down, but at the back of my mind I felt that we would henceforth need to temporarily lead our lives with extra precaution. In fact, all necessary permissions were taken for the event I had gone for. Besides, it was a small affair and was to continue for three days. The first day passed off peacefully. However, on the second day, we got a local municipality order that the session would need to be halted. Nothing like this had ever happened to me and neither do

I remember having left any session of mine halfway. I was unable to decipher as to what was happening. Could it be that everything was really changing? A trifle flummoxed, I returned to my home city.

Barely had a week passed, than our prime minister sombrely announced a twenty-one-day lockdown due to Covid-19. To be honest, I was completely shocked. I could never imagine how everything could be shut down as announced. How would people manage to not go out of their houses? How could they be prohibited to go out on the streets? Besides, it was said that no one could go anywhere save for emergencies. Somewhere my heart refused to believe this, and I was not able to swallow the happenings. I passed the next twenty-one days dreamlike, quite in denial of reality. Thereafter, I was hopeful that everything would soon open up. But the situation turned from bad to worse and the lockdown period kept extending. Never was I more stressed and traumatized, as I had never stayed away from work for such a long duration.

Seeing me troubled, my father told me something which was an eye-opener. But before I write that, let me take you back by about a year and a half. I had always been very keen to write something for a long while; things like the lessons I had learnt in life, my learnings and experiences—I wanted to gather them and put them together in one place. Yet, somehow, I never found the time, or maybe it was an excuse I would give myself. I would habitually tell my father that had I some more time I would write this and that, but it's unfortunate that I barely found time. A year and half passed me by spelling lame excuses. Now let me get back to what my father had said during the lockdown.

Seeing me stressed out, my father asked me the reason for it.

I told him, 'Don't you know?'

'My work has stopped!

'My going out has stopped!

'All my plans for the year are failing one after the other. And work having stopped, I barely know how I can manage to run my life which centred on my passion . . . my work! I want to go out to work; I want to recite my *kathas* and being stuck at home is causing me great distress.'

Hearing this, he calmed me down with great affection and said, 'Remember, you had told me some time ago, that you wish to gather all your lessons and experiences and write a book. Now you have plenty of time. Instead of feeling sad for not being able to do your *kathas*, why don't you try to write your book? If you think some of your plans have gone astray, why not do something that you hadn't planned before?'

Hearing this, all my troubles metamorphosed into strange excitement and enthusiasm. Time was showing me two pathways: one, where I had nothing else to do but cry and shed tears, because my work was put on a hold and nobody knew for how long, especially when for over fifteen years that is what I was used to doing. The other option being, I could do something new which I had never done before. I did not sleep that night. When I woke up the next morning, I chose the second pathway for myself and thus began a new journey in my life.

I must add here, while the idea of writing a book came quite easy, writing it out was very difficult. What I felt would be easy—in the sense that I would do it when I had time—took me five years to complete. I wrote a lot, then erased it, wrote again and then erased it again. Yet, at the end, I did finally manage to reach you through this book. It was all far from easy, but then doing something worthwhile in life never really is. Especially, when the happenings are completely different from what you had initially planned. Because there is a saying, if things happen as per your choice, then it's good, should it happen otherwise, then it's better. Because when things do not go our way, perhaps that is what God decries, and he is never wrong. I made my plans, but God had different plans for me.

So sometimes it is okay if your plans fail because the Universe has greater plans for you; all you need to do is—wait and watch!

The plans we make often fail
It makes us in traumas drown;
Know, the cosmos has its plans
It will never let us down.

16

It's Okay to Be Successful

There are times when we hear about a new restaurant opening and are told that the food and service are excellent. Soon the place becomes famous in very little time. After a few months, we begin to hear people commenting that the food and service was once good but the quality has since gone down. You too may have heard comments like these. Why do you think this happens?

Why is that we begin well but cannot keep up the tempo and later we lose our way? Because success is known to bring arrogance, it begets self-obsession, fair doses of superiority complex and even makes us tardy. Those successful begin to feel that the reason behind their success is because there is no one better than them. And that whatever they do—everyone will like and appreciate it. Here, one thing we must all remember—success is far more dangerous than failure. Reason being, should we fail to handle success, the speed with which it takes us to the top, it throws us to the bottom at double the speed.

Then how do we manage to keep ourselves sane when we achieve success? And what would be the best route when we attain great heights in life? When you begin any work, at that point of time, you work very hard, and with every honesty and diligence. And at all times, you strive to do something different and better. You also try to concentrate hard on how best to provide your seniors, customers, audience or clients. But can we regularly maintain such high thoughts and ideals, such selfless mentality and good intentions? In truth, we often fail on such points.

The moment our work and performance get better and begin to rank among the best, our hard work, our creativity and our enthusiasm start to wane and soon they take a back seat. We begin to feel that since we have name and fame, whatever we sell, people will seek it out and buy it. We falsely believe that our work having attained a certain level, the rest is easy. Barely do we realize that the real work and progress have just about begun. Remember, to be successful is perhaps not that difficult—many people become successful—but to remain successful is the hardest part. It is difficult, indeed, to stay perched on that elevated platform for a long time.

When people begin liking your work and efforts, know your real work has only begun at that point. Reason being, until you had reached this point, your attention was in the ratio of 50:50 (50 per cent upon your work and the rest on ensuring that people like your work). And now that you have attained that place, work should be focused on, at 100 per cent. For now, you have the option of doing what no one else has done before you. However, we take our success for granted, and that is the surest way to our ultimate downfall.

You need to remember, the more you attain success, the harder you need to work and the greater is your responsibility to add value to society. Only then will you be able to hold onto your position of success for a longer period of time.

So it's okay to enjoy your success but not okay if you take that for granted. It's a harsh truth: success can be both illusive and fleeting in your life. It only stays with you if you keep working for it like you did when you wanted it. Once you stop that, it passes to someone else. Someone who is more deserving than you and keeps working for it endlessly. Because we are not the only ones who can do a particular work or task well, there are numerous like us who can do it as well and perhaps even better. So the only way of remaining successful is to never let success get to your head. Keep working like you did when you weren't successful—and never stop—if you wish for it to remain with you.

Success comes and then it goes
Keeping it is no small art;
You need to invest all your life
Thus, seek it with all your heart.

17

It's Okay to Lose Some Friends

Friendship happens to be the most beautiful relationship of this world. Friends play such a crucial role in our lives, which more often than not beautifully complements other relationships. At times, we cannot share things with our parents, but we have friends; sometimes we cannot share things with our partners, yet have our friends, then at times we cannot share things with our colleagues, we still have our friends. We have our friends at all times.

Usually, friendships begin from our school days because our first friends are those we meet in school. Then we make friends while at college, and later at our workplaces. However, it is very rare that friends we make at the very beginning of our lives stay till the end of our lives. The reason being, as we grow up their number decreases. You may have also realized that the number of friends you had when you were a child is not as many today. Are they? The most common answer would be 'no'. As children we felt the more friends we have, the merrier life is. We had large groups of friends from school, from our tuition group and also from our building and neighbourhood. With every of these groups, we would have our doses of fun; sometimes it was a birthday treat, sometimes parties and sometimes play and fun, and such get-togethers, according to us, is what friendship was all about.

Then as we grew up, our friends began decreasing in numbers and the true meaning of friendship also underwent a sea change. When I was a child, I had some fifteen or maybe sixteen friends, as I grew up, they were reduced to some seven or eight. And now there are only three left, the ones I can truly call my friends. At the beginning, I would often think if this was alright. Was separating from friends and losing them, one at a time, normal? Am I making some mistake? Maybe, we all think in a similar fashion when our friends gradually decrease in number. The question arises in mind: why is this happening?

I have known people to feel sad and depressed after romantic break-ups, but I also wonder how come people do not speak about their friendships breaking up. Why do they not speak about a happening when a good friendship breaks-up in a single moment; especially those with whom they have made wonderful memories in our past? It takes time to digest such facts. It was no different with me. As we grow up, we realize that maybe those who were our friends are no longer friends, because our very meaning and concept of friendship has undergone change.

In younger days, friendship was about fun and frolic, but now it is more about peace and understanding. Once we mature, having a friend implies someone with whom we can speak with our hearts out, someone who can tell us the difference between right and wrong. Someone who tells us we are wrong, when we do wrong, but never tries to judge us because of that. And they also help us to correct ourselves. I always say in my sessions, that the youth nowadays are misinterpreting the meaning of good friendship. What he or she wants is that a friend is someone who will always support—irrespective whether you are right or wrong. But then this is not true friendship. One who allows you to walk towards a huge abyss and does not stop you—how would you call such a person a friend? Fun has its place but being forthright in friendship also has its place.

Now we are no longer children, we have grown-up, we have responsibilities—and the ones who understand this are our real friends. Sometimes they do not manage to connect for long, but when they do, it seems we only spoke yesterday. This is true friendship. Someone, who does not utter a word of praise in front of you, but behind your back speaks highly of you, is a true friend. In the process of growing up, when being with someone brings alive the child in you, is a good friend. Friends bring about a deep inner peace, and the ones who usher this feeling are true friends.

But not everyone is like that. Therefore, as we grow up, many are left behind in the hallways of life. And it is completely okay, for the ones we leave behind are perhaps not our real friends. And the ones who are really our good friends do not go anywhere. And as to who these are, you will only realize with time and age.

So, it's okay to lose some friends, but not okay to cling on to those who are not your real friends.

Friends are glowing butter lamps
They usher blessings and light;
They steer us past grave darkness
No matter how long the night.

18

It's Okay If You Look Different

Our looks and deportment are something that fascinate us from our childhood days. How to look beautiful and smart in the mirror, in photographs, in the eyes of others is something that keeps many of us busy for a considerable length of time. How should our skin be? How fair must be our complexion and what should be our weight? We spend half our lives listening to comments on such matters. Be it from our own family members or our relatives or maybe even from advertisements being shown on television channels. Everybody speaks about how you should look. But why does anyone not speak about how you should be from within? How long would this outward appearance matter? A person who looks good but is otherwise from within, how long do you feel they would successfully carry on with their work or manage their relationships?

I read a story some time ago, and it explained in very simple terms this complex subject. Once there lived a man who made a living by selling balloons. He would display and sell an assortment of different-coloured balloons: red, yellow, blue and purple. Every time his business became a bit sluggish, he would release a bunch of helium-filled balloons in the air which would attract children and they would flock to him and his sales would rise again. This he would do all day long.

One bright day, he felt someone tugging at his jacket and he turned around to find a little boy. He asked the boy, which colour balloon did he want? The boy replied that he did not want any but had a question. The boy asked the balloon seller, 'If you released a black-coloured balloon, would that also fly?' Surprised by the boy's question, he barely realized that the complexion of the boy was a little dark. He wondered at the fact, that how did society manage to bandage the boy's mind with its dirty labels? Yet, moved by the boy's concern, he replied with empathy, 'Son, it's the not colour of the balloon but what is inside that makes it go up.'

How you appear from outside or your outward appearance does not take you ahead in life; it is the qualities which you have within that take you forward. The balloon may have any colour, but it is the air inside of it which decides as to how high it would rise. It so happens when we find people who are more successful than us, we begin copying their hairstyle, start dressing up like them, eat their favourite food and even try our level best to look like them. But is it because of their hairstyle, their clothes, perfume they wear or the way they put their make-up and the food which they eat that makes them successful? The answer is a resounding 'No'. What takes them ahead is the manner in which they lead their lives, the principles and values they adhere to, the amount of hard work they put in and their grit in life which takes them ahead.

To make ourselves happy, we bedeck our outward appearance, which is fine and there is no harm in that. But should we try to make our inner appearance better assuming that the outward appearance would automatically improve? Because remember one thing—people don't only like you because of the way you look. And even if they do, it is going to be a temporary thing. People tend to like you because of the way you behave or treat them. Or for the good qualities you possess. Work on those, and you will definitely find yourself flying high in the sky.

So, it's okay if you try to look nice, but it is not okay if you think too much about your outward appearance.

Don't be taken in by looks
Something we have all been told;
Try and see what lies within
Whether it's carbon or gold!

19

It's Okay If You've Failed in Your Past

It so happened, a man was walking down a road when he noticed that a huge elephant was tied to a rope attached to small iron angle buried barely inches into the ground. He was utterly surprised that an animal of the strength and size of an elephant could possibly be held with a coir rope tied to an iron angle pegged to the ground. Out of curiosity, he asked the owner of the elephant, 'How have you managed to hold this giant of a beast with an ordinary rope tied to an iron angle in the ground?' The animal can with a single shrug sever this rope and be free.'

The owner replied, 'When this elephant was small, I would tie it down with this same rope and this iron angle pegged to the ground. At that time, it tried its level best to break free of the rope and uproot the iron-angle but failed as it was too small to do it.' Then he added, 'It tried this many times thereafter but each time it failed. Now I believe my elephant still thinks that the rope is far too strong for it to break free, for it has long stopped trying to break it or uproot the iron angle.

'The elephant has since grown. It is so strong now that it can tear this coir rope in no time. But its previous failed attempts are ingrained in its mind and those stop him from trying to break free. That is the reason why despite it being so big and strong, it is tied with that rope held by an iron angel pegged barely inches into the ground.'

Upon hearing this, the passerby thought, how some poor chapters in one's life have the inherent ability to spoil the entire story.

This happens to us too. We cannot somehow get over our past attempts and failures. They make us believe that we would make the same mistakes and would fail again. But we fail to understand that perhaps when we had begun years ago, we had little understanding. However, over the years we have gathered much experience and knowledge. Once we did not know what we needed to do. Now we are aware and also know how to avoid that mistake and knowing this—we can do better. Isn't that a boon?

An unsuccessful person is not one who tries and fails but is certainly one who never ever tries. In true measure, if you try to do some work or task and fail to do it, then how can it be concluded that you have failed? It is very possible that you have adopted the wrong method to do the task and that has failed. It implies that your manner and technique of doing it has failed and not you. Therefore, it is wiser to try a different method or technique.

Suppose when you are going somewhere and take a wrong route, do you sit down to weep because the route shall not take you to your destination? Would you do that? No. You would ask a passerby for help, so that you may find the right route. You even try to take the help of technology to help you reach your destination. At times, if you are to visit someone, you even call up that person and ask for the right directions.

So, you can try so many different ways in order to find the right way. If that be so, why don't you do the same when you lose your way in life? Having taken the wrong route, why do you jump to the conclusion that you will never find the correct path? Who knows, you may have gathered more knowledge and understanding than what you had in your previous attempts. However, like the elephant, you keep imagining that you are incapable and not strong enough to be able to break free and find your path. A thought that never allows you try once more. So in the end, who ends up losing? No one but you! Therefore, isn't it wiser that you attempt once more, break the shackles of the feeble rope and be free? And who knows you may find your path and succeed.

So it's okay if you've failed in your past, but it's not okay to drown in despair and never try again.

To fail and to try again
And never give up on life;
Is the surest way to win
Despite the struggles and strife.

20

It's Okay If People Can't Measure Your Progress

There was a boy named Harish, who loved running marathons. Over the years, he had participated in many marathons, but for some reason or the other, he could never complete a single one of them. One day, he came upon a hoarding announcement that there was a marathon being organized in the very city he lived in. He got very excited. Aware of his past failures, he promised himself that no matter what, this time he would finish it. It did not matter whether he lost or won, but he would breast the finishing line.

Soon the day arrived, and Harish participated as he had planned. He began running with the other participants. Soon he was running quite well. But in a short while he began to tire, so he felt it was better to slow down. He then slowed down his pace to a jog; however, he began to tire more and his speed slowed down further. He noticed that his fellow runners gradually began passing him by, one at a time. Seeing almost all the runners ahead of him, he stopped, clasping his hands on his legs, gasping for breath. It is then that an inner voice told him that he had promised himself to finish the race and that it was now or never. He decided to heed that voice.

Having begun in earnest he realized that he could barely run, so he thought at least he could try to walk. Braving extreme exhaustion, he began to walk towards the finishing line. Even that was proving to be very difficult for him, but he did not stop. At little further, he stumbled and fell and sitting on the ground he told himself, enough he should let it be. But again, a voice from within said that he had anyway lost the race, but if he did not finish, then it would be tantamount to losing to his own self-confidence, and there could be no greater loss. Nothing could be worse than losing such a race in life. With the last ounces of his strength, he stood up again, found he could barely walk, but with faltering footsteps he kept moving towards finishing line and ultimately finished the race.

In truth, Harish was no winner, for he had lost the race. So even though in the eyes of the world he was a loser, to himself he had proved an important point. He had certainly fulfilled a promise to himself for he had made progress in his marathon-running abilities.

This story gives us an important lesson that our real race is not with others but with our own selves. If you keep trying to race others and win, then perhaps you may not manage. Because someone or the other would be better, more talented and far more capable. You must have heard this from your teachers that there is always 'room for improvement'. Therefore, nothing which is achieved can be the best; it can always be made better. Similarly, when someone or the other is better, it's totally okay, but that is not your race in the first place. Your race is always making yourself better today than what you were yesterday. The measuring yardstick you have made for yourself is what you need to follow, not the ones laid down by the world. Your success will only be determined by yourself and not society.

I would love to quote something I had written in a similar situation: *Redefine success in your own terms, the world will adjust.* That day, Harish had lost as per the parameters drawn by the world, but had he really lost? The answer is in the negative. For the world was judging his performance by the last race he ran, but according to him, it was the only one he had managed to finish. So in his own eyes, he was a winner! Therefore, it is quite possible that the world is not able to see your victory because it is regarding you with different eyes. Your struggles, your hard work and perseverance are best understood by you yourself and not by the world. So it's okay if people can't measure your progress but not okay if you cannot see it too.

Let people say what they wish
And measure you as they may;
Be your own measuring stick
Better yourself, every day.

21

It's Okay to Be a Rebel

This chapter is particularly meant for every youngster, for many of them at a certain age turn 'rebels'. It is a very common trait, almost universal, and there is nothing wrong with it. When children become teenagers, they go through some very important physical and psychological changes. It is an in-between stage, when we are in the cusp of childhood and adulthood. On one hand, there is a deep-rooted sense of insecurity, vulnerability and self-doubt, and on the other, there are signs of abrasive defiance to mask that sense of insecurity and other shortcomings. To give you a visual imagery, that period of our lives is like that of a ship that has raised its anchors from the seabed and is passing through a turbulent stretch of water before it can lower the anchors again.

During such a phase many people find it hard to adjust with their surroundings. They have difficulties in maintaining relationships and listening to elders. Their resistance to obey orders is often accelerated by insolence. In such times, we even treat our parents and guardians as enemies. We grudge and grumble in our own little bubbles, thinking, 'Oh! Why doesn't anyone even try to understand *me*?'

This feeling is quite natural at that age. However, as we grow up, we all begin to understand our parents better. We begin to understand how vital and precious their company is. But more often than not, it gets a bit too late before we understand this truth. Let me tell you a story to explain.

One fine day, a father and son visited a kite-flying festival. The young boy was excited when he saw the sky filled with colourful kites. He asked his father if he could have a kite and some thread on a roller so he could fly a kite too. The father found a shop in the park where the festival was being held. He purchased a colourful kite and a roll of kite-string for his son.

His boy was very excited, and even more so when his kite climbed high up in the sky. After a while, the boy said, 'Dad, it seems the thread is preventing the kite from rising higher. If we cut the string, the kite will be free, and it will rise even more.' At this the father cut the thread from the roller and the kite rose high in the sky... that made the little boy very happy!

But then, slowly, the kite started to swing down. Soon it fell down on the terrace of a nearby building. The boy was surprised and disappointed at seeing this. He had cut the kite loose from its thread so it could fly higher but instead, it fell down. He asked his father, 'Dad, I thought after cutting off the thread, the kite would be free to fly higher and higher. Why did it fall down?'

His father explained, 'Son, when someone is at the height of success in the life they are living, they often view other people, their families, their responsibilities and obligations as things that prevent them from going further or being more successful. The thread for the kite was not preventing it from going higher; it was helping it stay higher even when the wind slowed down. When the wind picked up again, you made the kite climb higher in a proper direction with the help of the thread it was attached to. Later when we cut the thread, it fell because it lost the support we were providing the kite with the string attached to it.'

The boy realized his mistake.

The moral of this simple story is that sometimes in our life while we move ahead in life, it appears to us that our close relationships are a barrier to fulfilling our dreams. Had we kept away from them, perhaps we could have made more progress, but in truth your family, your near and dear ones and your friends are like the thread of the kite that holds onto you. They are like your roots. Now, can being away from the root help to make headway? The answer is an obvious 'no'. Until you stay rooted, you will keep moving ahead and grow. The moment this connection is broken, it may quickly take you further up, but remember, it will bring you down with the same speed. And in truth, what is the benefit of attaining great heights, when none of your near and dear ones are around to celebrate the success with.

Growing up is often a tedious process in life. And every child passes through a plethora of experiences, especially when it comes to their family and elders and their varied exchanges. Sometimes children rebel and are unwilling to accept the advice of their parents and guardians, but it must be remembered that a strong foundation is so important to build a high-rise. This is exactly what a family and our parents do for us, just like the kite and its string, so that we can rise as high as we wish. It is also fine if at times we find their advice unwanted and even intolerable, for many things cannot be learnt but only experienced. Finally, it is okay to be a rebel if you have a valid reason behind it and it is adding a greater value to your life but not okay if that rebel nature is forcing you to remain unwilling to value the pearls of wisdom our parents and elders share with us.

Roots our families provide
Is an edifice to rise;
It helps us remain buoyant
A truth let us all surmise.

22

It's Okay If People Say Bad Things to You

Once Gautama Buddha was giving a discourse in a small village, and people were listening to him with great attention. Discourse over, a young man marched in and began to abuse and accuse the great saint in a nasty tone. Buddha took no offence; on the contrary, he kept smiling. At this, the young man got angrier and began using harsher words, the decibels of his tone rising. Buddha remained calm and did not utter a single word to him. At this, the man asked Buddha, 'I've said so many bad things to you, but how come you remain unaffected by my harsh words? How come you don't feel bad? How is it that you don't feel angry at what I have said? And does it not occur to you that you should shout or tell me something or even get me beaten up?'

Buddha smiled benignly and spoke for the first time since the man had walked in upon him. 'Answer this question of mine. Had you brought some gift for me and I would've refused, then with whom would the gift have remained?'

The young man sarcastically replied, 'What a question! This even a child would have answered. The gift would remain with me.'

To this Buddha said, 'Exactly, the things you are trying to give me—in the form of bad words, abuses and accusations—are quite like gifts for me. And I refuse to accept them in the first place. Therefore, all your abuses, your allegations and your profound negativity stay with whom?'

In deep thought, the man replied, 'Naturally, they would remain with me.'

To this the sage replied, 'Now if I have not accepted any of these gifts, then why should there be anger or repercussion about something I never accepted.' Saying this, he departed from there.

Always remember, Buddha is not a persona but a mindset, for to remain calm under the most intimidating of circumstances is being like Buddha. If we can bring ourselves to do this, we would all be happy and peaceful.

This story imparts a vital wisdom to us about life: people keep telling us many things. Sometimes they are admonishing us about our work, at times it's about our looks, during other times they simply try to relieve themselves and purge their anger upon us. However, these things can only trouble us if we accept it. Should someone state you are a bad person that does not make you a bad person. It is only when you accept what they comment about you, that you endorse their opinion. Let me give you an example. Suppose you are walking on the road and someone calls out your name. You would turn around to see. But if that's not your name, would you turn around? Similarly, should someone criticize you unnecessarily or insult you for things you haven't done, you shouldn't respond. If you want to keep yourself happy, do not react to what people tell you. If you manage this simple task, half your troubles would be over.

So it's okay if people say bad things about you, but it's not okay if you react upon their remarks and make yourself miserable.

To remain calm and peaceful
Is a blessing—undefined;
Take not to heart pronging words
People are all of a kind.

23

It's Okay If You Feel Stressed

Stress is part and parcel of our lives. Every person experiences stress sometime or the other, and at times on a regular basis. There are several things that can stress us out. There is stress when you are trying to do something really difficult. There is stress when you meet a personal loss, or things just don't move the way you planned them. Unfulfilled desires and wants, too, cause stress. But the problem is not with such issues; to have stress is commonplace, but to remain stressed is not normal. Let us try to understand this through an example.

Imagine you are holding a glass of water in your hands. Hold it for a minute, there will be no problem. However, if you hold it for an hour, it may cause some discomfort. But if you hold it for an entire day, your hand may become numb, and your discomfort may increase. The weight of the glass of water doesn't change over time. Therefore, it implies your discomfort was not because of the weight of the glass. Then, what was the reason? The real reason was, the longer you hold it, the heavier it becomes. The stresses and worries in our life are like that glass of water. If you think about them for a short while, it may not make any difference. But if you think about them a little longer, it will start giving you problems. And, just in case you think about them all day long, you will feel paralysed. Hence, it is not about problems coming into your life, but it is not doing anything about them which gets troublesome.

We often tend to think that the life of others is easy and all the world's problems are ours. But this is not true. You must have heard of this adage, 'the grass is greener on the other side.' In truth, the grass is greener on that person's side who waters it daily. Here watering means, dealing with the problem, working upon it and trying to solve it; for problems come to each and every person. When you imagine someone has no problems in life, it is a fallacy. For problems plague them too. The difference being that they spend time trying to work on it and solve it, rather than complaining about them all day long. So, such a person does not try to hold the glass full of water in his hands, but either throws the water or puts down the glass.

And when you begin working upon your stress and try to sort out your troubles, somewhere you are also trying to make yourself stronger to face the challenges of life. No one knows what life might suddenly throw at us. What may be a glass full of water today may become a jug full of water tomorrow—and even worse, a tank full of water the day after. If one cannot handle a glass of water, then how is it expected that one would manage a jug or a tank of water? Therefore, the best way to deal with stress is to face it head-on and work to solve it.

So, it's okay to feel stressed, everybody does, because that is how life is, but it's not okay to keep feeling that way and not do anything about it.

Stress is filth heaped in your mind
Which must be cleaned every day;
Should you allow it to pile
Miseries will crowd your way.

24

It's Okay to Change

You must have heard this line many times, from your friends, from your colleagues and from your partners and also at your workplace, 'Now you have changed', 'Ah! You have changed so much!' or 'You weren't like this before.' Such lines sound very negative to us. What this means according to them is that we are no longer as good as we were before.

But this is not true or correct at all times. As we grow older, we undergo many changes. The first being the bodily changes, which we try to accept with great grace, and we try to find beauty in ourselves. Also, try to be comfortable with such changes. But then why don't we give this kind of support and acceptance to our behavioural changes, emotional changes and intellectual changes? For when changes happen with age and responsibilities, why do we not take them positively?

We all know that change is a natural process. We can even say that change is a proof that we are passing through a learning and growing process. With age, you experience many things; some good and some bad. Some break you and some make you. You go about understanding what is right and what is wrong. Based on that you create your boundaries, you change your behaviour, your patterns of working or just being the way you are. You become selective with the people you allow to be around you, you let go of old habits, you let go of some relationships, your friends sometimes and that is for sure not an easy journey but you do it anyway because you know that is for your own good and that is a very courageous thing to do.

If somebody is not able to understand that then you should definitely vacate that space. Reason being, if someone cannot accept the positive changes in your life, then that relationship is perhaps not right for you. It could be any kind of relationship. Could be someone from your family, a friend, could be your partner, even your colleagues. If someone likes you because you are following their way of living, their likes, their standards, something which makes them happy, then there is something deeply wrong. For if you do things without their consent even once, and thought about your own issues, your own feelings, about things that made you happy and the way you want your life to be, along with your own responsibilities, your own learning, your own growth and it makes them feel that you have changed, you should know that it is one big red flag. They are not your true well-wishers.

Your real friends and well-wishers are those who celebrate and appreciate the good changes in you, because even they know that in the journey of life, change is another name for growth. Even the Bhagwat Gita says that change is the only constant. And the one who does not change with time is the one who suffers the most. So it's okay to change if that change is for your own betterment, but it's not okay to feel guilty about it.

Change is one great truth of life
We must learn to accept it;
Be it 'bout us or the world
It is change that keeps things fit.

25

It's Okay If You Want People to Like You

I really like you!
You look so good!
You are amazing!
You are the best person I've ever met.
You're so beautiful!
You're so funny.
You're glowing.
You are so intelligent . . .

We love listening to such lines—such encomiums that come our way sometime or the other! It could be from a parent, sometimes from a teacher, more often from a friend and also from someone whom we take as very special. And to hear this, we work hard on such qualities that we may attract such comments. At times we help people, even try to make them happy, then there are opportune moments when we try to complete some work for them. On occasions we try to be funny, and dress ourselves up, and do this only with the hope that people like and appreciate us.

Nothing is wrong in this thought: for we all like the fact that people like us and appreciate us. The problem is when such thoughts become our *need*. If you make yourself better and then expect appreciation and also expect others to like you, this is to an extent okay. However, when this attitude becomes more than a mere want and we get addicted to such comments, it is then that we tend to do anything to attract such remarks. Irrespective of whether the work we do is good or not.

I have seen people who are in the habit of talking about others behind their back, tattling and even sharing people's secrets they know with all and sundry. Do you imagine that people do this because either they dislike someone or wish ill of them? Surprisingly, that is not always true. They do it either to attract attention or to be liked by the person who we are with. But are such acts correct? Is depraving yourself to be liked by someone a fair act? I don't think so. We do such acts, lose our own personality just to get ourselves liked and appreciated by others. The truth being, how long would they like you—is there any guarantee of that? Quite possible that after a while they may even begin to dislike you. But by then you would have demeaned yourself so much that getting back to your original personality or self becomes extremely difficult.

We do not come to this world to impress others, but to live our very own lives. More than working towards trying to make others like you, you must work hard to improve yourself in order to make yourself likeable to your own self. Always remember, the manner in which you develop and grow your personality also attracts and helps connect with people who match that. If you are nice, good people will automatically like you. And should one not like you even then, perhaps they are not good people in the first place.

So it's totally okay for people to like you, but not okay to be miserable when they don't. Because real confidence is not about whether people are going to like you always; it is actually about being okay even when they don't.

It's fine to be loved and praised
When people speak well of you;
But stooping low to snatch praise
Will never fetch you your due.

26

It's Okay to Be Materialistic

One day a saint boarded the first class compartment of a certain train and embarked upon a journey. He carried with him some belongings which were carefully packed in a number of bags. An affluent trader too boarded the same train and took his seat right next to the saint. Much like the saint, he too, had a fair number of baggage. No sooner did the train leave the station than the two began a casual conversation.

The trader, looking at the saint and the bags belonging to the saint commented, 'You see that there is little difference between us except for our apparels.'

The monk looked surprised but let the trader continue without interrupting.

'We both are carrying a fair number of bags and somewhere we both seem to be almost on the same plane except for our clothes.'

The monk still did not comment. A short while later, they disembarked at a small station where the train stopped en route. The monk insisted that they share a cup of tea to get rid of their tiredness. The trader agreed and while they stood at the platform sipping hot cups of tea, the guard blew his whistle. Upon hearing it, the trader began to sip his tea quicker so that he could finish and board the train. Then as he began to walk towards the train, the monk held his hands and asked in a calm tone, 'While we were on the train, you mentioned that there is little difference between us, isn't it?'

However, the trader was restless and replied, 'Can't you see our train is departing? We can discuss this after boarding.'

The monk smiled and held the trader's hands and said, 'What's the hurry, friend? There will be other trains on this route and we will be able to complete this journey.'

The trader, surprised at his remark, quipped, 'That is fine, but you forget my belongings are lying in the train.'

Despite the trader wanting to quickly board the train, the monk was unwilling to let go of his hands and unhurriedly replied, 'Oh! But so are mine.'

The trader, now struggling to free his hands, almost shouted his response, 'Now I have understood what you are saying. While we both are in the same first-class compartment, with almost an identical number of baggage and going on a similar journey, you have no attachment to your belongings, while I can't let go of mine. And that is the difference I did not understand earlier.' Then he jerked his hands free and ran with all his strength to board the train, which had by then picked up speed.

What is this story trying to teach us? Nowhere is it being said that you need to let go of your things or belongings. No wise person will tell you that only upon leaving everything you will get happiness because happiness is not attached to anything or any object; it is something we manufacture within ourselves. Which one can feel in all circumstances. Otherwise, why is it that those who have everything are unhappy, and the ones who possess nothing are also equally unhappy? The problem is not with your belongings, your dreams or your possessions, it is in your own self. You must understand when and where you need to draw a line. It's never about owning something; it's about something you own which begins to trouble you; that is the real problem.

Have you ever seen a lotus flower? If you observe carefully, you will see that the water droplets on it can be clearly seen. The reason is that the flower does not accept them; it never lets the waters around own it, even though astonishingly it grows and remains in the water. We sometimes behave the opposite with things and belongings and get so attached to them that our own happiness and sadness get inexplicably attached to them, which is absolutely unwarranted. Luxury and a materialistic life are to give you comfort but are not meant to usher in happiness for you. The day you understand this difference, you will truly understand how to remain happy.

So, fulfil as many of your dreams as you can, and if, to improve upon your ease of living you want to buy your favourite things, go buy them. But remember when you buy things, it should not be the other way around, that they in turn end up possessing you. For the day when objects begin to buy you out, your happiness will come to an end. So it's okay to possess materialistic things, but not okay if they begin to dictate terms on you.

Possessions can bring no joy
For attachment begets pain;
Be a lotus in water
And blessedness you shall gain.

27

It's Okay to Be a Good Person

Recently I happened to be in Benaras, waiting for a shoot to happen. At a little distance I noticed a middle-aged man sitting with a few children around him. He was regaling them with stories. Somehow the child in me came alive, and soon I too became a part of that group of children. I began listening to the story the man was sharing with them. The story went like this:

Once a poisonous snake happened to slither into a small village and took shelter there. Thereafter, whenever it felt threatened or endangered it would attack the villagers and even bite them. As a result, quite a number of villagers were bitten and some even died. The villagers were terribly upset about it, but none dared to go near the snake for the sake of their own life. It was around that time that a sadhu came visiting the village. The villagers, having paid their respects, related the tale of the poisonous snake and the terror it was causing. They told him, that they feared he would bite many more and was perhaps hiding somewhere nearby, waiting for an opportunity to strike.

The sadhu possessed certain supernatural powers, he even possessed the ability to talk to beasts and reptiles. By the dint of his inner vision, he found out where the snake was hiding. Then nearing it, he commanded the snake that henceforth it should not bite anyone in the village. The snake promised to obey. The sadhu told the villagers that they should not worry any more and that the snake would no longer trouble them.

The storyteller then paused and carefully considered the expressions on the faces of the children. Satisfied, he continued with a smile. To be honest, quite like the children I, too, was intrigued and was left wondering how it would end. The man continued:

Exactly as the sadhu had assured them, the snake never bit anyone thereafter. The fear of the reptile completely vanished, and nobody bothered about the snake any longer. To a measure that while children played, they even pelted the snake with stones the moment they set eyes upon it. Such incidences would badly injure the snake, yet it did not bite anyone, as it had promised the sadhu.

Time passed by and the sadhu visited the village once again. Having come upon the snake, he noticed that it had several injuries and seemed badly wounded. The sadhu approached it and inquired about its pitiable condition. The snake replied, 'My condition is a result of your command to never bite.' It added, 'Ever since I stopped striking, the villagers began treating me poorly and never missed an opportunity to hurt me.' The sadhu remarked, 'You foolish reptile, I stopped you from biting but not from hissing. Had you been hissing at them when they tried to hurt you, they wouldn't have managed to harm you in the first place.'

The story made me realize that being good does not mean that you allow others to take undue advantage of your goodness. If you do not try to resist people who constantly try to trouble you, you only give them a long rope. That is not goodness; that's mere stupidity. A good person necessarily means someone who knows his or her boundaries. A good person never steps out to trouble anyone but should anyone cause them trouble, they respond to it adequately. What needs to be marked here is that the response of a good person will always be most dignified and adequate. If a person stoops down low, it is not necessary that we, too, do the same and make a poor example of our own selves.

To take an example, if someone uses foul language with a person and if that person is a good soul, it is obvious that they would not respond with abusive language. However intimidating the circumstances, a good person does not forget their dignity and principles and knows how to respond within their parameters.

In the story you just read, the sadhu had forbidden the snake to sting but never stopped him from hissing at his abusers. Therefore, one's behaviour should be such that the person across should comprehend that while you do no wrong, you will also not tolerate any wrong done by anyone. Only such a person is called a good person. Therefore, it is time you change the definition of goodness you have learnt. And I feel this is a vital lesson for us.

That day, the children happily left having heard the tale, and I am very sure they would soon forget it. For certain things can only be learnt by experience, and considering their age, I knew it would take them years to fathom the real depth of the story they had heard.

But I did, and it further dawned upon me that a person who has no self-respect and dignity cannot be called good. A good person is one who assists and helps the good, raises their voice against wrong and injustice. Also, such a person values self-respect above all else. Here, one must be aware that if you allow some atrocity for the first time, then perhaps it is the mistake of the wrong-doer. However, should it be allowed to happen again, then it is completely your mistake. So it's okay to be a good person but not okay if you allow another to take advantage of this rare quality. For then, it would not be termed as 'goodness' but sheer stupidity.

The good aren't meant to be weak
This they ought to understand;
They must guard all who are good
And lend them a helping hand.

28

It's Okay If You Are the Only One Doing It

Let me begin this chapter with an interesting story. Once there was a severe drought in a village, and the villagers were suffering untold miseries. Crops had failed, animals were dying and there was literally no food left to eat. The distraught villagers were seeking solace when a holy man happened to pass by the village. Upon hearing their plight, he offered them a remedy. He commanded that on a particular night, every family in the village send a member to visit an old, dry well that stood outside the village precincts. There they should pour a mug full of milk into it. He also mentioned a condition: that the act must be done when it's completely dark, and no one visiting the well must either look into the well while pouring the milk or look back after having poured the milk. This would beget blessings from the rain gods and it would surely rain in a few days. The holy man having left, the villages planned to do exactly as he had advised.

Thereafter, every family began planning to collect milk so that they could pour it in the well. However, one family thought differently. They felt, if everyone was carrying a mug of milk on a dark night and were forbidden to even look into the well, why not carry a mug full of water. With every family pouring milk into the well, what difference would a mug full of water make? So on that particular night, the villagers went to the old well outside the village and each emptied their mug. They waited for a few days, then the days turned to a week, but it did not rain. It was then that the holy man once more appeared and the villagers asked him why it had not rained. To this, the holy man took them to the old well and asked them to peep inside. The villagers stood shocked, for in it there were no traces of milk, the floor was soggy with water.

In truth, every family thought similarly: that their pouring water would not make a difference, considering the others were pouring milk. Seeing the bottom of the well, every villager understood the reason. It became clear that every family in the village had cheated on what they had promised. And the miracle did not happen as promised, for everyone failed to do what was said by the holy man.

In life, if each of us thinks how would it matter if I alone don't do it? then perhaps the situation would resemble that of the dry well, where at the end there would only be water and nothing else. Often, we shirk our responsibilities or avoid our work thinking that someone else would do it, but how does one know that the other isn't thinking the same. And we must remember here that change does not come about when the whole world begins doing it; it happens when we ourselves begin to do it. The greatest gamechangers on this planet have always been a handful who began to do things all by themselves.

The freedom fighters we read about are not ones who began with large teams or groups of revolutionaries; they began their journey all by themselves. Seeing their bravery and sacrifice, a crowd gathered behind and their numbers swelled every passing day. Had they too thought, what difference would their singular effort fetch, perhaps we would have never attained freedom from British rule.

These again are rather extreme examples. I am by no means asking you to fight a war at the border.

All I am saying is, we can at least try to make the place where we live a little better. Who knows, someone may feel motivated by our effort. Now, be it keeping the neighbourhood clean, helping someone or maybe even encouraging a good habit, the initiation has to be done by our own selves.

Remember that it is futile to speak about something that is not good or acceptable, but far better to speak about something that is good. If you don't like something in this world, then instead of cursing that, why do you not act and do the opposite. In doing this successfully it is better you prove to the world that, even today, it is far cooler to be good! That is how you bring about the real change.

Ranting does not bring about change, abusing the country will not usher change, speaking ill of others will not bring about a change. Abusing and demeaning society will not bring about change. Change happens when we climb down into the quagmire of affairs and clean it with our own hands. And if you do not have the courage to clean it, then you have no right to call it wrong.

So, it's time you bring about positive changes, even if you are alone at it. Things may appear hard at the beginning, it may also take time, but if you are right, the time will come when the whole world would rally behind you. So it's okay if you are the only one doing it but not okay to quit because you feel you are alone, and that the effort would be pointless.

To take up for a good cause
Something not many can do;
Needs courage and a brave heart
And it gives its rightful due.

29

It's Okay to Have Problems

Everyone desires a stress-free life. They feel if all their problems were to go away, it would automatically make their life stress-free. And it is because of problems that their lives are replete with sorrow. But is this really true? Who does not have problems in life? Can you name one person who is free from problems? It is impossible. There are those who, despite their problems, manage to find some happiness, while there are others who get overly stressed with only a single problem in their life.

My mother told me a story when I was very young. It remains imprinted in my memory. Whenever I face problems, I remember that story:

Once, there was a young girl who was faced with quite a few problems during her teen years. So much so that she was unable to come to terms with it and would often remain sad and depressed. Finally, one day, unable to handle her problems, she approached her father, whom she was particularly fond of. She elaborated the difficulties she was facing. Upon listening to her, he explained a phenomenon. 'Just imagine that you have three vessels with water in them. Now you place each one atop a stove and let the water get hot. While it does, you put some pebbles in the first vessel, coffee beans in the second and potatoes in the third. Let the water boil and observe the changes. You will see that the vessel with the pebbles will not show any changes happening to the pebbles. However, the vessel with the coffee beans will show that the water changes in colour and texture. The position will be quite different in the vessel with the potatoes. For the potatoes would change texture and become soft.'

He then went on to explain, 'We must learn to alter our reactions depending on the situation we face, that is, in life we must and may need to react in different ways depending upon the situation. The pebble is hard and unyielding and hence remains unchanged. The coffee beans are completely yielding; hence form a new identity fusing with another. Whereas the potato reacts differently—it becomes soft and therefore edible.'

Here, we need to understand that all three were soaked in hot water. This implies that trying situations and problems come to each and every person. But what matters is how you react to adversity in your life, and such reactions will determine the changes in your life. So the first wisdom is that you need to determine your reaction to the heat and whether you will be a pebble, potato or coffee bean. However, there is another pearl of wisdom hidden in this story—perhaps you can be all three. The only thing being you need to understand when and what you need to be.

If in a certain situation, you feel that you should not react, then it is similar to being a pebble. Now it can also be that you may need to alter your own self in certain situations and fuse into the situation. Here, you will be like coffee beans that mix with water. Again, you may feel it better to be like a potato and need to handle the situation with some softness. These are decisions you need to make. It is quite possible that you may not have any control over the hot water, but what you may become as a result of being soaked in it is very much under your control.

The sad part is, we always tend to focus our attention on those things over which we have no control. This is the reason why most people remain unhappy. In truth, they must learn to focus their attention on things they can change and upon matters they can live with. The day we take charge of the gear of our life, from that day onwards we will notice positive changes. And till the time we give the control of these situations to external elements, we will remain stressed; it matters not if we have and possess everything.

It is not the problems one has but how one reacts to them which ultimately counts. So, it's okay to have problems but not okay to feel perpetually stressed about them and do nothing about changing ourselves to sort them out.

Stress drinks the sweetness of life
Drowns us in pain and sorrow;
We ought to face it with grit
Thus, wisdom we can borrow.

30

It's Okay to Not Get Married

You all must have heard this phrase—'It's okay to arrive late than to arrive ugly.' My question here is: What if I don't want to arrive? What if I don't wish to be a part of this party?' Will that be considered okay? Will that be considered normal? Because society has planted some rules in our minds in such a fashion that breaking them seems akin to committing a sin. We feel if we do not do the things everyone else is doing, then perhaps society will not accept us. With a result that they would then view us with different eyes—a thought that can trouble us considerably.

In truth, society comprises and is composed of us. Such rules and regulations are only made with the sole objective that our lives are smoother, easier and more purposeful. So that it brings a lasting kind of peace into our lives. If a rule does not bring us these benefits, then not adhering to them and sometimes changing them is needed for the well-being of all. Among such rules, one is 'marriage'. Which, as per societal protocol, one is bound to adhere to. An institution you are supposed to be a part of at a certain age or else society does not consider you 'complete'.

We are told and made to dream about our marriage since the time we are very young. Some habits are imbibed in us for the reason that they would prove useful after we get married. I can still remember instances when as a child I would end up arguing with my parents. They would retort, 'You can fight and argue with us as much as you desire but remember, you will not be able to do it when you are in the house of your in-laws.' Also, 'Here at home you wake up so late, but there you wouldn't dare do that,' and things like that.

And not just parents, I recollect that even our relatives would often say, 'If you keep doing such things, then who will marry you?' 'If you do that, then how will you manage your married life?' Come what may, everything somehow seemed related to matrimony. 'You need to study hard so that you get a decent marriage proposal.' 'You need to be good-looking so that you get a good partner.' 'Your behaviour should be refined so that you can enjoy a happy married life.' Everything pointed towards marriage, as if the final and end goal in life is nothing but marriage! Therefore, like many others, I too began to feel that unless I am married, my life would remain incomplete.

I still remember when I was in Standard XII, I would tell all my friends that the moment I graduate I will get married and settle down. For that is what I had heard all my life; that marriage is all about settling down. And to be very honest, who doesn't want to settle down? But as I grew older and began to mature, I began to understand that marriage is not about settling down. It is about spending the rest of your life with someone you love. Sharing your life with him or her; sharing your happiness, your sorrows and your highs and lows; when you can be your real self being with this someone special. Marriage is certainly not what is shown to us in movies. It is far more challenging and difficult than that.

One question would always haunt my mind, 'What if I never got to meet that person whom I could love so much that I would wish to spend my life with that person?' It is not necessary that everyone finds that one special person they can care about. What if they do not find this person? Would it be fair they get married to just anyone and compromise on their life's desires. Most surprisingly, many in my family and close circles said exactly this: that no matter what, some compromises have to be made in life, for not everything we wish for, we get. However, I could never digest such talks.

While I work, I meet people, many of whom are of my age; I have realized that questions which milled inside my mind were in the minds of many. There are some who never found their right partners. Again there are also those who are not even searching for a life partner. Because they feel that they do not need anyone to either make them happy or to feel complete. And somewhere this is probably right. Why would we want to get married? So that it could usher some joy and peace into our lives. If we feel that having married, we may not be in peace or derive joy, and furthermore even lose the peace and joy we already enjoy, isn't it better that we abandon that very path which leads us to such a mess? Because rather than there be two sorrowful persons living together, there be one person living happily by himself or herself.

It is high time we understand that not everyone is trying to find a partner. There are some people who are busy trying to find themselves. They wish to know more about their own selves. They wish to discover themselves and also want to love themselves and they are happy with their existence and wish to live their lives alone. Also, they get a lot of peace in their solo existence. Then why should someone ruin their peaceful state of mind and existence just because society 'wishes' otherwise? We hear folks warning that there are disadvantages to being and staying alone. Then are there no disadvantages of getting married? Do problems not come to married people? And don't they make an effort to solve the problems as and when they arise? Therefore, those who stay single by choice and have problems will surely find solutions to their problems, too.

I am nowhere advising that you should not get married and stay single, but what I mean is that it is not about being married or not but all about doing what makes you happy. And if marrying someone makes you happy, then you should do that. But if it doesn't, you shouldn't. So it's okay to not get married, but not okay if you do it because society feels you should. Remember, at the end of the day it's your life and therefore the important decisions should be yours. Reason, if that goes wrong, it is you who will suffer and not society. Remember, people will pass comments and move on with their lives, but the one who will need to bear the consequences life-long would be you!

To get married or not to
Is a choice so hard to make;
Should be made for your own ease
And never for others' sake.

31

It's Okay to Have Flaws

Nowadays, the following phrases have gained almost unreflective currency in our society. They are:

It's okay to have flaws;

You don't have to be perfect;

Accept your flaws.

Up to a measure these phrases seem to be okay. But I think a little differently about those phrases. Some may not like my thoughts on this but do hear me out for once. As it goes without saying, when we embark on anything, we hope for the best. All our ideas and actions in their initial stage, generally speaking, are driven by good intentions. As we progress upon them, many factors arise and our course of thought and action may take unexpected turns. New events keep on influencing our earlier thoughts, so much so, that at times our initial intentions go astray. We feel short on our intended aspirations and achievements.

The phrases I've mentioned above often come along at such moments of felt inadequacies. It's perfectly okay not to be acutely self-critical. It's perfectly okay not to be too harsh on ourselves. We don't have to beat ourselves up to be perfect because no one is. The first step is we have to accept our flaws. But what is meant by 'accepting my flaws'? Simply put, it's about accepting our mistakes and not heaping blames on others or passing the proverbial buck.

What after we realize what our fault is? Is it okay to gratify ourself by saying 'It's okay to have faults? Or should we make efforts to rectify our mistakes? Correct our course of action?' One has to remember that we do not live or work in isolation. Many people are attached or linked with the life of almost every individual. They can be family, friends, partners, colleagues, customers and all kinds of human relations. The point I want to make is: Why should anybody else suffer because of our faults, mistakes and indiscretions? Let me give you an example, and this is a very common one. We all have seen people who are simply unable to control their angry outbursts. They go berserk over something trivial and hurt people for little or no reason. If there's sufficient cause for annoyance, then perhaps it's okay to become annoyed. But unmanageable anger is generally regarded as a personality flaw (like people with vindictive traits) and that needs to be rectified.

There's another side to this argument. Though we are happy to justify our own flaws by saying it's okay to have them, we are rarely generous when it comes to accepting flaws in other people. Isn't that pure selfishness? While self-love or loving oneself is a good trait, selfishness isn't. A self-loving person accepts their faults and tries to improve themself every day—mentally, emotionally and physically.

If you really try to understand my opinion, then you will comprehend that I am not against anyone having flaws. For having flaws is perhaps God's way of saying that we have a greater scope of learning and growing in life. Please do not shut that door by saying that you are okay with keeping that flaw. Because that is how you put a full stop to your own growth. So it's okay to have flaws. But once you know you have a flaw it's not okay to nurture it and do nothing about it.

To possess flaws is human
There is none who has not one;
To nurture them all life long
Is a sin under the sun.

32

It's Okay to Be Rich

Who doesn't want to be rich? Everyone wants to have money. People wish to go on a world tour; they want to buy their favourite things. Nearly everybody wants a big house or a fancy car. However, not every one of us can actually realize such desires. While we all aspire to be wealthy, only a few can attain great wealth. The great artist Pablo Picasso had once famously quipped, 'I'd like to live as a poor man with lots of money.' Incidentally, Picasso himself was fabulously rich.

The question I'd like raise here is: Is being rich just about having plenty of money? Indeed, money does help to purchase things and services, and it does pay our bills. But can money alone make us happy? I've seen many people sitting on mountains of personal riches and yet have little peace or satisfaction. They are wealthy, indeed, but are they happy? Hardly so.

In my opinion, if you really wish to become rich in life, then you need to become affluent in the four things I mention below. Only then will you be able to truly call yourself rich:

1. ***Spiritual Well-Being:*** According to me, this is the greatest wealth. This is because it works according to your inner wellness. What is the benefit of being wealthy if your intentions, your thoughts and the manner of your working are wrong? How many days can you remain happy with that kind of wealth? Always remember, a thief is scared of even his own shadow; it matters not how much he earns by robbing others. Shall we wish for such a life? Can we go far with impious thoughts and intentions? And just in case we do reach somewhat far, shall we really be able to enjoy our wealth in a carefree manner? The answer is a resounding 'No'! We will always be worried and scared that someday people will discover the truth. The facade will break and our real intentions shall be revealed.

Would you like to live with such fear, all your life? I don't think so. So if you really want to work on something, it's important that you work on your thoughts, your intentions and your mindset, so that you turn into a better person. Spirituality does not take you away from money; it makes you mentally and emotionally strong so that you can utilize that money for the right causes. If you have an instrument you do not know how to use, then it will be no good to you. Spirituality enables you to use that instrument in the right manner.

2. *Physical Fitness:* Everything in our daily affairs seems important for us, until the time we fall sick. It is then that we realize that nothing is more important than health. What is the point of going crazy trying to earn money, all the while ignoring our health? And then when it's time that you wish to enjoy that money, you are compelled to use it to pay hospital bills in order to recoup your health which you knowingly destroyed in your prime years. Both money and success are best enjoyed when one is in good health.

So in our busy lives, we must learn to give priority to our health. Otherwise, we may begin with a bang but end with a whimper.

3. *Relationships and Family:* A happy family life is extremely important for anyone to do good work. But these days how many of us devote enough time and care to our families? Yes, I know many will point out to their weird office schedules and accompanying professional pressures that are increasing day by day. But is that all? Isn't it true that with proper time management and understanding we can take out some time (however little that may be) on a regular or almost regular basis to buy some time for our near and dear ones?

   We may earn money, carve out a name for ourselves and even reach great heights professionally, but what is the point of such success when we have none of our near and dear ones beside us to rejoice with? We all know that we don't only work hard for ourselves; another important reason or factor is our family. And we endeavour to work hard, day and night, to give them a good and comfortable life. But then what is the point of being so busy if you have no time for your near and dear ones? I'd suggest not to waste the present in trying to give them a good future. Remember, no one has seen the future. I am not saying that you do not plan for the future, but in the midst of such planning and work, you ought to find some time for them *now*! Or else how would your family remember you? That you spent your days running about like a train engine! Had no time to sit with them, talk to them and spend time with them! Would all this then really be worth that trouble? Think hard. And remember, a time will come when you, too, will crave for the company of your family. I have seen instances where a person found no time for his family in his heydays, thinking he had all his life to give them time. Later, when he was at the fag end of his life and finally thought he had the time, to his utter dismay found that he had no family left to be with him. So, think hard about prioritizing your family.

4. ***Financial Freedom:*** Money is important. It may not be the most important thing in life, yet it is very important. If you desire an easy

and comfortable life, then you need to have money. And you have to work hard for it. Let no one fool you with the words that money is not everything in life. Money can do many things in life; the only thing you need to know is how to utilize it well. The wrong usage of anything can make it most negative. This is the reason why at times we look at money in a very negative fashion. But money is never good or bad; it is people who are. Therefore, try to earn in the best possible manner, invest and use it in the right place to bring comfort into your lives. And whatever we let go during our childhood because we had no money, let us fulfil those desires. One must have money in the first place to be able to say that money is not everything in life! Today good education, good health and fine living require money. And which youngster would not love the idea that with his or her money, their parents would live a good life? Therefore, work hard, earn well and use your earnings wisely.

Improve in all the areas mentioned above and you will find that there is none richer than you in this world.

For today, many people may be found with money, but they have no happiness. So always remember, it is okay to be rich, but it's not okay to think that only having money makes you rich because it doesn't.

Money may not make you rich
But peace, health and bonding will;
Garnish them with healthy thoughts
There can be no better pill.

33

It's Okay to Have an Opinion

Let me begin with a beautiful story that I often relate during my kathas. Once a man was travelling by train with his twenty-year-old son, and a young couple happened to be seated in front of them in their coupe. The young man sitting near the window shouted out to his father, 'Dad, look, there goes a tree.' The couple found this very odd for the boy was too old to exclaim like a child, but they ignored it. After a little while, the youngster once again shouted excitedly, 'Dad, see, what a beautiful bird!' Now the couple found the fellow not only childish but also strange to make statements you'd expect from a child in kindergarten. After a short while, he once again exclaimed, 'Dad, see, those feathery clouds there.' Now, the couple could no longer contain themselves. It made them remark in a mocking tone to the father of the youngster, 'Why don't you consult a doctor for your son?' The father smiled and said, 'That is exactly where we are coming from. You see, my son was blind from birth. It is after a prolonged treatment that he can now see. So, whatever seems very ordinary to you happens to be most extraordinary and wonderful for him.'

How quick was the couple in opining about the young man. Which they did, without thinking, without knowing anything about him and without understanding what was going on in his life. But don't we too behave like this sometimes? Do we, before judging someone or gossiping about someone, try to find out something about their life? Maybe about their difficulties, their struggles and also about their past? Perhaps we don't? Whatever we see in front of our eyes moves us to pass judgements as if we have this intrinsic right to interfere, air our opinion and give unsolicited advice to other people.

For once, let us take a lesson from this story. What if the father of the young man told the couple—'My son hasn't said or done anything to you. So, mind your own business.' Why don't we think for a moment before we pass judgements on others? Why is it that we are almost always taking personal digs at others about their personal lives, looks and even career choices?

Let me ask you, are we running their houses and paying their bills? If the answer is in the negative, then howsoever they are conducting themselves should be none of our business. It is high time we understand that until our advice is not sought, and until our opinion is not wanted, it is better to keep it to ourselves.

We often stoop low to criticize or embarrass people about whom we know nothing. And such harsh criticism often enters into areas where, in order to criticize, the critic has to have some expertise. Many of us enjoy watching cricket and are really passionate about the game. I have heard people airing opinions in public about an experienced professional cricketer of international repute on how he could improve upon his game! I wonder how many of those critics are technically competent to pass breezy comments on matters that require not only a thorough knowledge but also tremendous effort and hard work. Trolling on social media has become quite a fashion these days. Members of trolling brigades usually know very little about what or whom they troll, and how it affects the people they target. It's not constructive criticism which they indulge in, and it helps no one.

While being judgmental about people we often forget to understand their immense contributions in their chosen field and fail to understand how hard they have worked to climb up to the position they have reached. Despite the fact that we have not even achieved 1 per cent of what they have, we have the audacity and supreme confidence to comment about how they should be conducting themselves. Is it, therefore, not better that if we are keen to comment on someone, we must try to say something nice and positive about such a person, rather than be derogative in our behaviour? And in the case it is someone we know, and we happen to meet them, we ought to behave nicely with them, appreciate them and conduct ourselves in a manner that they feel good about it and leave us feeling pleasant. Would doing this cost us money? The simple answer is 'no'. But in the current times which are often negative, it helps bringing about a touch of positivity. And the reason for it would be you. What could be more beautiful and satisfying? And just in case you do not like someone, it's better to avoid such a person and keep away from them. But saying something wrong and controversial about this person would not be tantamount to doing something positive in this world.

Remember, if you cannot say a few good words, it is far better that you say no words at all. Each one of us is fighting an unseen or unknown battle in our lives; therefore, we must avoid making the lives of others more difficult or unhappy by passing unwanted and unwarranted remarks. So it's okay to have an opinion about somebody, but not okay to speak it out unless it is asked for. Because every person in the world has their own story. Avoid judging people before you truly know them and also because the truth might surprise you.

We may have our opinion
To speak them may not be right;
For we know not 'bout others
And battles they need to fight.

34

It's Okay If You Are Ambitious

I was always very ambitious as a child. I wanted to be the best in whatever I did. I was not sure about what I wanted to do in life, but all I knew was that I wanted to do something so unique that I could feel proud of myself. I wanted to carve a niche for myself in society and also try to bring about positive changes in society from that platform. Till date, despite traversing a long way, I have lost none of my ambitious spirit. And perhaps it is this very spirit that keeps motivating me to do something special and remarkable in life.

Some time ago, I had gone to an engineering college for a motivational session. The topic was 'How to Balance Success and Spirituality'. The reason for this topic could well be that fact that perhaps almost 90 per cent of the youth would be thinking on these lines. The session was most fruitful, but the moment it concluded, a young girl came up to me and volleyed a plethora of questions:

Is it bad to be ambitious?

Is it wrong to dream big?

Is it wrong to want to do something spectacular in life?

Is it wrong to try to make a name and space for myself in society?

Am I to remain satisfied with whatever I have?

Am I being greedy if I want more in life?

Am I being less spiritual if I want a comfortable and happy life for myself?

I was looking closely at her face while she asked these questions, and I could see the sparkle in her eyes as she spoke of the life she dreamt of. But what I also noticed was the streak of worry which had spread out on her face in the midst of these aspirations. Somewhere in that young girl, I could spy the 'Little Jaya' who had the same set of questions when she began her spiritual journey. After listening to her, I asked her a few questions myself.

'Whatever you wish to do, that which would make you successful, would that work be considered as good work?'

She replied in the affirmative.

Then I asked her another question, 'Would someone benefit from that work?'

She responded, 'Yes, many would gain from it, and their lives would get easier.'

I then asked, 'Is it also your dream that you wish to do good for the society and bring out a positive change?'

She replied in the affirmative.

I smilingly replied, 'Then you are already on the path of spirituality, my girl.'

I waited for the girl to absorb what I said then continued, 'Spirituality is not about leaving everything and living a life of a recluse; it is all about having a higher level of awareness, and if you have that, it will help you considerably in your ambitions. It won't steal your ambitions or your dreams. The reason being, if everyone forsook everything, then how would society function? How would businesses run, how would the country run, and in what fashion would society move forward? Now imagine: engineers, IPS, IAS, life coaches, therapists, MBAs, leaders, teachers, motivational speakers, entrepreneurs, doctors, architects, politicians, who would man these posts and positions? Now imagine if each of the persons manning these important and high positions work only to benefit themselves without tempering it with a touch of spirituality or higher consciousness, then where would the world go—in a better or a worse way?

The girl replied, 'Obviously worse.'

I concluded, 'Hence, there is nothing wrong in being ambitious and it is certainly not counted as greed. And on the day your ambitions are not balanced with a measure of spirituality, you would turn from being ambitious to competitive. Then instead of trying to fulfil your dreams, instead of trying to bring a positive change in society, you would spend time competing with others. And you would only waste yourself in trying to go ahead of someone else. And in trying to bring yourself on the top, you would try to bring someone else down. This would lead you to the path of greed.' With that the girl seemed satisfied and left having thanked me profusely.

I wish to conclude this chapter saying, you cannot bring yourself on top or succeed by bringing others down. You cannot win if you are trying to make someone lose. In trying to accuse or give someone a bad name, you cannot prove yourself to be right or get a good name. If you indulge in all this, your dreams will never come true. They will only come true if you work honestly and hard by focusing on your own goals. Therefore, dream of whatever you wish to dream about. Achieve whatever your heart desires, earn as much you wish to. But remember that it must be the effort and result of your honest efforts.

So, remember one thing. It is not at all wrong to be ambitious, it is not wrong to want more in life; it is not wrong to have bigger goals but remember to add that pinch of spirituality or should I say a higher level of consciousness to your life. And you will see how great a life you will make for yourself and for the world. So it's totally okay to be ambitious, but it is not okay to be competitive. It is your journey and it should always remain like that. The day you start comparing your success and life goals with others is the day you turn your ambitions to competition and then to greed.

Ambition is good for you
Know dreamers are never small,
Work hard for a better world
Then it's a win–win for all.

35

It's Okay to Have Expectations

It is normal for people to have expectations; everyone has them. It begins the moment we are born. Even if you have observed an infant, who knows little about this world, the baby would have umpteen expectations, though the baby's life has hardly begun. The baby has limited requirements, limited relationships, and also very few needs and the infant has not even begun to dream, but yet the expectations have grown. For example, if you eat in front of this baby, watch its face closely, the child expects that you would feed it too. Also, the child would be expectantly looking at the door waiting for its guardians and parents to return home in the evening. Now imagine when this child grows up, would the expectations decrease or increase?

It is very normal that expectations will increase significantly. This is a natural process and nothing is wrong with this. All of us want something in return from somewhere or the other. We work so that our purpose is fulfilled, get bonded in relationships so that we find and get love, earn money so that we can usher comfort into our lives, and many more such things. There is nothing wrong in doing these things. But not being able to handle these things well can really play havoc with your life. So let us try to understand some of our expectations from life and how to handle them:

Expectations from life goals: Expectations from life can be a powerful motivator. It helps us to become better, do better and behave better in life. However, it can also be a source of stress and disappointment if they are not managed well. It is natural to want things which make our lives comfortable, which makes us happy and gives us power, name, fame and money. But life does not often unfold as we imagine of it. Sometimes we want things, and they never happen in our life. And at times, to our utter dismay, it runs in the opposite direction. In such situations, what should we do? Here we have two pathways. First, we can begin despairing that whatever we wished for or expected did not happen. The other pathway is we handle the situation in an attitude that perhaps what has happened is for the better, and we would get something much more than what we had expected or imagined.

Now don't you feel the second path is a better way of handling the situation? But in reality, do we do it? No, we grudgingly accept defeat and become despondent. We decide not to work any longer and quit from trying to attain our goals. Here many may think that the second path is easier said than done, and it is true, choosing the second path will not be easy. It will in itself be a difficult decision to take. But nothing in life is easy; every aspect of life can be difficult. I'll quote a few examples:

—The lives of those who don't have work are difficult; and those who have work find it difficult to handle it;

—Those who are unmarried, find it hard to live by themselves; and the ones who are married find it hard to manage their matrimonial life for a prolonged period;

—If people have no money, they find life very stressful; and those who have enough of it find it hard to maintain financial discipline.

There are numerous such examples which point to the fact that life is not easy, and that perhaps it is meant to be difficult. It is about choosing which difficulty we desire, which difficulty we feel would make our lives better.

Expectations from love life: Do we all not want a happy and fulfilling love life? Yes, we do. Someone with whom we can enjoy our life, share our happiness and sorrows, and celebrate every phase of our life. And also to make a family when we choose do so. Is it wrong to have expectations from a person we choose to love? For example, if I love someone and that person claims to have feelings for me, is it wrong to expect a good measure of love, care and respect from that person? No, it isn't. That is the reason why we seek companionship, so that we can cherish our love and togetherness. But when that does not happen, then what is the way out? Thereafter, saying that it was not right to expect such things, would that be a correct thing to say? The answer being, obviously not. It is heart-breaking indeed. The one we love, expect loyalty from, and want care and respect from such a person, is that a wrong idea? And when you don't get it, the best step is to stop blaming ourselves and thereafter deciding not to stay in that relationship. Isn't that a better decision? With the conclusive thought that the person you were with is not capable of giving you what you expect and deserve. And the one who does not manage to give you the basic needs of a relationship, how would such a person manage to love and look after you? Your continuing in this situation may continue the relationship but not love. So the very reason of your expectations not being or getting fulfilled is a sign that you are not in the right relationship.

Expectations from society: All of us expect something or the other from the people around us. Be it our friends, relatives, family or colleagues. Because at the end of the day, each one of us is doing something or the other which in some way makes a certain contribution to the affairs of society. And to be praised for that contribution would not harm anyone. But this does not always happen, sometimes even if we do very good work, we do not get fair or due appreciation for that. It also happens when, instead of a word of appreciation, we are heaped with criticism. It is important for us then to remind ourselves that we are not working to make people happy. To do well to the world is not to make the world happy but to keep a certain inner value system intact, which makes one happy and content. Don't try to destroy your goodness in the face of poor and bad worldly behaviour. We are doing good to keep our own behaviour and values intact. Your goodness should never be dependent upon people's reaction and attitude. If this should this be the case, your goodness will remain until they stay happy with you, or else it will fail. Which is far from being the correct attitude. My goodness reflects my behaviour and beliefs and their attitude and behaviour reflect theirs.

Have realistic expectations: The three points mentioned above are some important expectations we have, which almost everyone has. But along with these expectations we come across quite a few instances in life, when we expect something or the other. At that time, we must remember that it is not wrong to expect if that is realistic. We cannot live in a dreamland. We must understand this about life and the world, we must also try to understand the situation we find ourselves in, at the same time we also need to estimate our own abilities and then set our expectations.

A person can have many thoughts and aspirations. But do we have the patience and ability to attain them? And should our expectations not materialize, then do we have the capacity to control our feelings and emotions? If your answer is yes, then please go ahead. But in most cases, our unrealistic expectations just fail to materialize. Therefore, it's time to give it a good thought.

So always remember, it is okay to have expectations, but it is not okay if you do not know how to handle yourself when things do not meet your expectations. Because life is not about what you get from it but how you handle it and what you make out of it in every circumstance.

Expectations are common
They're found in the hearts of all;
Often when they are belied
It gets tough to take a call.

36

It's Okay to Stop for a While

I was listening to a song a few days ago and the lyrics of that song compelled me to think about something. The song sung by the famous singer Late Jagjit Singh, is called 'Koi Fariyaḍ' and it goes like this:

'एक लम्हे में सिमट आया है सदियों का सफर, जिंदिगी तेज़ बहुत तेज़ चली हो जैसे'

In English, it implies, a moment holds the journey of an eternity, while life seems to have slipped away fast and then faster.

Having listened to these two lines, my life of twenty-nine years seemed to flash by right in front of my eyes.

In this race of life and living, we sometimes forget to pause or stop. We never find time to sit and analyse whatever we are doing and does that make us happy?

Did we always want to do what we are doing? The people who are near and close to us, did we imagine that they would be near us? Could it be that in this relentless running, we have somewhere left behind our loved ones? All those things we possess today, is that what we wanted from life? Or could it be that while living up to the expectations of this world, we clearly forgot our own wants and desires?

It often happens that by the time we have thought about such things, we have already gone far in life. And what remains is purely regret and we get nothing more out of it. Then we are left with laments that I wish I had paused a little that day and savoured those times. Wish I had enjoyed those moments a little more then. It would have been nice had we stopped awhile when crossing a few select people in our lives. Ironically, every one of these thoughts turns to 'I wish . . .' By the time we get to comprehend the true gravity of these thoughts, we realize that we have actually gone far ahead in life, so far that we have no time left to fulfill any of those 'I wish I had' thoughts.

Sometimes stopping for a while helps us relish the most beautiful moments in life; sometimes not doing something brings untold joys. Sometimes sitting in complete silence with someone feels better than spoken words. At times, savouring a favourite meal all by ourselves leaves the real taste of life in our mouths. It happens while trying to achieve great heights in life, playing a long-forgotten game from our childhood, momentarily brings back our wonder years. I will repeat, sometimes stopping awhile makes everything right. So it's okay to pause for a while but not okay to regret afterwards. It's important to choose the moment when we can stop for a while and savour a few moments of joyous fulfilment.

If life's piled with so much care
That we have no time to spare;
In rushing we spend our days
Be sure it will bring despair.

37

It's Okay to Have Power

I find it a blatant lie when people say, 'Oh, I get angry very fast. This is a problem that I have; otherwise, I am a nice person.' And many while reading this chapter must be thinking that indeed I have this issue in my life. But whatever I have understood about people, I find very little truth in these statements. Because if people really have anger issues and it is truly beyond their control, then it would reflect upon everyone. However, most people burst into anger but not before seeing who the person in front of them is. If the one in front is an important or powerful or influential person, who may be of use in the future, then there they stay absolutely quiet and will not exhibit their anger. However, when they find the person is subservient to them, perhaps dependent upon them or someone close to their family, then they do not hesitate to vent their anger. Later they remark, you know I have anger issues. I have witnessed quite a few of such situations in life and some of them have imparted a lesson I am now writing about in this chapter.

One day, I was sitting in a 'Coffee House'. Somewhere behind my table, a group of friends were chatting. One of them said, 'Today my boss scolded me for no reason, when it was not even my fault.' I felt it could be that the person's boss was angry due to some other reason, and unable to pour it out there, he took it out on his junior, knowing the fellow would not reply back. The youngster then added in a vengeful tone, 'The day I become the boss, I will show everyone who I am.' Listening to him I wondered if power makes us look at others in a lowly manner. And if having power is not about using it to bring about some positive changes in society but used instead for taking revenge upon others. A few months passed by and I kept thinking about what I had overheard that day at the café. Then I happened to read a story about Nelson Mandela, which compelled me to realize that my thoughts were not entirely wrong.

The story goes like this:

Once after he was elected President of South Africa, Nelson Mandela was having lunch with his security guards at a restaurant. Everyone placed their orders and were chatting away waiting for their meal. At that moment, he spotted a man sitting right across his table, also waiting for his order. He told his guards to ask that man to join them for lunch. The person agreed and joined them, but he sat quietly. When the meal arrived, everyone relished the food and the man ate too, but his hands were trembling. The man quickly ate and left. Everyone thought perhaps he was not well. Later, Mandela clarified that he knew the man. He was the jailor of the prison where Mandela was imprisoned. While at jail, he behaved very badly with Mandela and gave him a rough time and tortured him. But life had come full circle, and now Mandela was the President and could have done anything to that jailor. He probably felt that Mandela would have his revenge. But Mandela was a different man and refrained from such lowly behaviour.

This story proves that with 'great power come great responsibilities'. Having power does not mean that it is an opportunity to fulfil our vengeance. It does not imply that once we have power, we should use it to take revenge for the wrongs committed against us. Its true implication should be that whatever wrong has been done to us should not be repeated with anyone else. That day, Mandela could easily have taken his revenge, but that would not have elevated him to the heights he is known for. Because your designation does not make you great, your ideals, your behaviour and your contribution in making society a better place are things that make you truly great.

So, the next time if something wrong is done to you or something bad happening with you, remember that you are not to take revenge upon the person doing it to you, but you reach a plane where you can set right what was wrongly done to you. So it's okay to have great power, but it's not okay if you use that power only and only to fulfil your own desires and extract revenge.

Trees which are laden with fruits
Are known to bow to the ground;
Should power spawn not meekness
It will wreak havoc around.

38

It's Okay to Feel Jealous

A story comes to my mind as I begin writing this chapter. It happened right in front of my eyes, and goes like this:

Once during an annual college festival, there were a variety of shows being performed by the students. When it came to dancing, Priya, a girl from BA (First Year), performed and set the stage on fire. The hundreds of students present could not stop applauding her, absolutely awestruck with her performance. All the while a girl named Rashi, who was from BSc (Second Year) was keenly watching the performance in the audience; she too applauded vigorously when the performance ended. However, seeing Priya dance away to glory, she felt extremely envious. Rashi wanted nothing more than to be appreciated and applauded like Priya; she also wanted to get unfettered adulation.

Without thinking further, the moment Priya got off stage, Rashi jumped onto the stage and began dancing as the music came on. Rashi danced with much fervour for a few minutes but was clearly out of sorts, as she was not a good dancer by any measure. Soon, the crowd booed her and began hurling explicit comments, which caused Rashi much embarrassment. Realizing her folly, she hurriedly got down. She heard many a foul remark from the audience thereafter and a few students even heckled her for being on stage performing without practice or skill. Rashi was overwhelmed with guilt and shame at her stupidity. She then went backstage and began to weep. Finding her in a sorry state, Priya came to her and began to explain that she ought to have done things she was good at. She added that everyone had some talent or the other and whereas dancing did not seem to be her forte, surely something else could be. At this, Rashi replied in an irritated tone that she too wanted the same adulation but had failed, which had left her embarrassed in front of the entire college.

Priya asked her to calm down and advised her, 'You go home and think hard about what you are good at. It will take time, but you will certainly know it.' Without arguing further, Rashi went home. Much later, Rashi told herself that she would never again make such a mistake in her life. She promised herself that she would do things to entertain others in which she was naturally good at.

Here, Rashi had begun quite well by applauding Priya. It is not unnatural to feel a little envious when we see someone performing well. Because almost everyone wants to do something special, perhaps it is not a bad idea to become a little envious as it might inspire us to stretch ourselves a bit to improve. But by carrying this envy forward, Rashi made the cardinal error of equating Priya's dancing talents with her own. Just because Priya was good at something does not imply that the people who watched her on stage were also good at it.

Rashi did not understand this simple truth and tried running the race to beat Priya. Without understanding as to what her talent and interest was, she jumped into the fray and was acutely embarrassed. Had she tried to motivate herself after seeing Priya's dancing skills and endeavoured to do something well by herself, something she was good at, then perhaps she would have won the same adulation. She mistakenly used envy (which had a shade of jealousy as her motivation) and that had brought her disgrace, and she lost the race poorly.

Seeing someone else do better and thinking that you too wish to do something good in your life too and wish to make progress is not wrong. This kind of benign envy does help bring about a kind of motivation in our lives and sometimes it also helps us to reach our real goals. But in case you find someone doing well and you begin to feel why that person should be doing well and that it should have happened to you, you are envious in a malicious manner, and that brings in negativity which then becomes a de-motivator instead of a motivator and a source of inspiration. Such feelings, at the end, will not take you anywhere but will result in the person across you having poor and negative feelings for you. And since you have taken this in a negative direction, it begins to give bad results. Often it might happen when we wrongly attach a person's success to our failure. When in truth, their life is not in any way linked with yours. Their doing well has no bearing upon your work or life. But this feeling of malicious envy will not only bring an adverse impact in your life but also be a catalyst in spoiling your relationship with others.

You should not try to do what others are doing; try to do things that you are good at. Do what you are good at so that if you work very hard at it, you would never chance complaining about it. People attain success only when they act in such a manner.

So it's okay if seeing someone else doing well for themselves makes you feel a little envious, and if that feeling motivates you to do well in your own life. But if that feeling compels you to run a race not meant for you and makes you feel bitter against those doing well in their life, induces you to be negative in every situation and leaves you feeling sad, then something is grossly wrong with you. Also, if seeing someone else doing well makes you cringe within, then it is not envy but may be jealousy, and that is not okay. Such feelings should be immediately controlled and quelled. For instead of cradling it in the heart thinking it is the most natural feeling, remember at the end the one harmed will only be you.

Jealousy is disguised as
Envy with a friendly mask;
Wear it and you have trouble
Fair bit more than you may ask.

39

It's Okay to Be Lazy

In today's world to live a perfect and affluent life seems to have become the order of the day. The in thing being that one's clothes must be stylish and one needs to be updated about ongoings in the world. One should be aware of their physique. Also, the way one's figure should be and how many marks should be scored in examinations. To add to that, the kind of job one should have and what should be the salary. Not to forget the amount of time one spends on the internet and how to become productive. Such ideas go to an extent, as to where should one go for a holiday and how many parties to attend? All these need to be pre-decided. And strangely, everyone is supposed to follow the same puppet rules. Ones who do not follow such rules are either lagging behind or are plain lazy and sloppy and are even considered to be irresponsible and useless.

In truth, such kind of perfection can only be attained by a machine, perhaps only a robot can do things in this fashion and with such precision and measured time. But we are neither machines nor robots. The flaws we possess within make us human. Sometimes not doing things on time may also be good. At times not being productive and wasting a day is also considered fine to an extent. It is also not a bad idea to avoid a party during the weekend and spend that time catching up on sleep. Running a fine race is wonderful but also being a little lazy and not running one could be a good idea.

By being lazy, I do not mean that you stop working altogether, and that you do not take care of yourself and make no effort to improve yourself. Sometimes being a little less perfect is absolutely fine. Our life is not some race we must win at all costs. It is a journey we must undertake and while at it we ought to conduct ourselves in a manner and style of our own liking. So at times if one does not feel like doing some work and wants to go slow or be lazy, there is nothing wrong with such a thought process.

In this fast-paced life, not doing things on a particular day, avoiding working hard, not receiving any phone calls, avoiding speaking to people or not bothering to dress perfectly does not relegate you to the back bench. On the contrary, it enables building energy reserves which one could use for work thereafter. Imagine if every day is the same work and routine, then won't life become boring?

So while it's okay to be lazy sometimes, it's not okay to run like a machine just because society expects you to be perfect all the time. A little bit of a mess does not harm; it rather makes us human. Therefore, be a human, not a machine.

Fine being lazy sometimes
Good to have an easy day;
Know we do not live to work
Must find time to rest and play.

40

It's Okay to View Life Differently

Life is not the same for everyone. All have eyes to see things, but everyone does not have the same view of things. And perhaps that is the beauty of life: that each one views it in a different manner, which is largely composed of our own experiences. But sometimes by trying to compare and contrast our thought processes with others we end up staining it. It is then that we fail to see the true beauty of life. To explain this better, let me tell you a story I read quite a few years ago. It carries a deep lesson and it changed my perspective about life to a great extent.

One bright summer day, a wealthy man decided to take his son on a trip. The destination was a poor village far away from their bustling city life. The man's intention was to expose his son to the harsh realities of poverty and hardships. They arrived at the village just as the sun was setting, casting long shadows over the humble huts. Upon arriving, the man took his son to a farm, which was home to a poor farming family. The son observed the family carefully over the next few days. He noticed that the farmer and his wife worked day long in the fields, growing their own food; he also noticed the simplicity and hard-working lifestyle. 'Look at their dogs,' the son pointed out to his father in glee; the family owned four dogs, they ran around the farm all day wagging their tails and keeping watch. The son noticed that there was a river flowing by the farm; the family bathed and even washed their clothes in the river. Observing that the family grew their own food, the son remarked, 'How on earth do they manage to grow their own food?' The father quietly listened to his son's observations. The son also noticed how the family was surrounded by friends and neighbours. Late one night, the man, expecting his son to acknowledge their own privileged life, asked, 'Did you see how poor they are? What did you learn today?' The answer surprised him. 'We have a dog, they have four. We have a swimming pool, but they have a river, we need to buy food, but they grow their own. We have security and gatekeepers to protect us, but they have friends and neighbours,' His son said this all with a thoughtful expression on his face, and then added, 'Thank you, Father, for letting me understand how poor we are.' The father was stunned, for he had expected his son to recognize their wealth and understand the hardships of poverty. On the contrary, he realized that his son had found richness in what he considered a state of poverty.

This story explains that happiness is not always in the manner in which people view this world, but sometimes it comes from having a different perspective about life. Instead of seeing problems everywhere, we must also try to see the abundant blessings that surround us. We must try to observe what we have instead of what we do not have. We need not run along the path, society, people and life in general are running on. If God has given you a different perspective in life, perhaps he intends to make you do something, something no one else has done before. It is important that we do not let this opportunity pass. Rather, we must try to use this diverse perspective in bringing about a change in our own lives as well as to that of others.

You must always remember that not everyone will understand this outlook of yours. You may even face some difficulty when your own family does not approve of your views and vision. In that case, you need to be patient with them, explain your perspective and tell them that it makes you happy and in the long run that would be most beneficial to you. Yet, if they refuse, you must persevere in the face of every obstacle. The world-famous epic of Mahabharata is replete with remarkable examples in this context. Remember, time and tide will prove that you were right. One who wears dark glasses given by the world will never understand the vision of your soul. But that is okay, it is not for you to make everyone understand this subtle difference.

Sometimes, the true beauty of life can only be viewed and seen by a select few. Like they say, only a jeweller can know and understand the value of a diamond. In the same fashion, should you want a life akin to the glow of a diamond, you need to be a jeweller with a profound outlook on life. So, it's okay to sometimes view life differently, but it's not okay to change this outlook because society refuses to understand and acknowledge it.

To have a diverse outlook
And vision others have not;
Might make you seem a rebel
But this battle must be fought.

41

It's Okay to Be Bad in Someone Else's Story

In our lives, we meet many people. Some are close to us and there are others with whom we don't share a special relationship.

Every one of them has in their hearts and minds an image of us. Now this image may have been created by what they assume us to be or it could also be that the times we have spent with them have painted the picture. It could also be the result of some memory you share with them. Whatever be the case, everyone keeps an image or memory of yours. Sometimes, this image may be a good one and conversely it may also be a poor one. We need to remember that we have no control over this thought or image. This is perhaps one reason why it is pointless to care too much about what others think of you. It is quite possible that at times what they think of you or what they imagine you to be, you are not that kind of person at all. Despite this, you waste your precious time upon such frivolous thoughts.

What people think about you is their business. You can hardly do anything about it. As wise people say, you can lie down for people to walk on you, and they will still complain that you're not flat enough. Therefore, it is better that we live our lives on our own terms and measures. Needless to say, as long as there are people around you, they will say something or the other. No matter how much care you take or whatsoever you may choose to do, there will be those elements in society who will discover faults in it, and if there are none, they will invent some. Therefore, I wish to tell you that it's totally fine if they do so.

There is one more thing you need to understand. I am in no way endorsing wrong behaviour, rudeness or abusiveness, and neither am I trying to justify someone's intentional crass conduct. I am only saying that being kind and respectful, and to remember one's limit is proper even by today's standards. No matter how much this world has changed or changes, no matter howsoever modern it becomes, certain things will forever remain in fashion, like being kind and thinking good about others. It happens that sometimes some people are not nice; they are villains in someone else's life, but one fine day their karma catches up with them. Because even if the Gods forgive them, their *karma* will never do that, for they will find a way to get back at them and extract their dues.

What I am hinting in this chapter is that sometimes we are not wrong, our intentions are not wrong, but in trying to make others happy, we end up sacrificing our own happiness. Such acts of ours put them into a poor habit of expecting far more than they should. And if we think about ourselves even once, such acts somewhere, somehow paint us in poor light in someone else's life. Given such a situation, to be labelled as bad is appropriate. In order to make others happy, and in trying to do so, throttling our own happiness is not an appropriate thing to do. In trying to make someone else feel superior, should you need to make yourself feel inferior? If so, then that is not a space you must tread into, for it is a poor idea.

Also, while trying to respect others, we must remember to not lose our own self-respect and dignity. But this demeanour comes with a price: we might end up losing friends, losing relationships and some close ones may end up distancing themselves.

But you need to decide as to what you want in your life. Do you want a life where everyone is happy with you, but you are not happy from within? Because you have spent your entire life in trying to love others, making them feel comfortable, sacrificing your own happiness to give them theirs and living up to their expectations in a fashion that they may like you. Or do you wish for a life where without intentionally hurting others, you spend time trying to keep yourself happy, working towards fulfilling your own dreams and keeping your own self-respect elevated. And for this state of affairs, it matters little that we will be deemed bad in someone else's story. Are you willing to take that risk? The choice is yours.

I would like to end this chapter with this quote, 'The day death comes upon me, it will be me who will die, and no one else will die on my behalf. So until I am alive, let me live as per my own will and thoughts.' So it's totally okay to be a villain in someone else's story but not a good idea to be one in your own story. So be true to who you are, and then watch the real good ones celebrate your authenticity.

To be bad in someone's tale
Is far from bad after all,
To be villain your own
Can be the most tragic call.

42

It's Okay If You've Done Something Bad in Your Past

I am not perfect!
I am only human!
So if I make mistakes,
Read the first sentence again!

Yes, we all have done things in our life about which we feel no pride. We do not feel nice about it and to add to that even carry a sense of shame that we did it. In truth, every one of us has done some wrong or the other, be it with our friends, times in our life, with our family or perhaps with our life partner. Sometimes even with a stranger. But the guilt over those mistakes can become paralysing if it consumes us. If we do not try and cure this feeling of guilt, it can demoralize us. Should we try and understand this aspect of our lives well? Yes, we can try to make our present and future better. Here are some simple solutions by which we can overcome this feeling:

To try and understand the situation: Sometimes it so happens that we don't intend to do wrong, but our situation doesn't give us a choice. And here our inner self knows the truth that whatever we are doing is wrong. It is then another voice that speaks from within, it justifies that there wasn't a choice. Therefore, between two wrongs, what could have been possibly chosen? It may also happen that at times we don't even have the liberty and time to think about our choices. It does not allow us an opportunity to analyse our actions, whether they are right or wrong. This does not mean that you do not consider the wrong as wrong. But cursing yourself for it all through your life is not proper. Because you never intended to do or commit that wrong in the first place. Sometimes a person is not wrong, but his circumstances are bad. Therefore, trying to understand the situation gives a greater clarity and prepares us adequately for similar situations which may arise in the future.

Acceptance: Though we understand the situation, it so happens many times that we try to defend our own mistakes. We console ourselves that it was not our mistake and that the situation was compelling. On the contrary, we must explain to ourselves that whatever be it, a mistake has been made. And whatever we have done was not right. In addition, we must also understand that whatever has been done cannot be corrected. Whatever has happened cannot be changed, but we can always acknowledge our own mistake. There is no need to prove ourselves right by dint of force. Otherwise, that guilt will never leave us. Reason being, to correct anything, we first need to admit that it is or was wrong.

Apologize: Most times, whatever wrong has been done, we can do little to correct it. But with whomsoever we have done wrong or in someone's life something bad has happened because of us, we can always seek forgiveness from such a person. Be it with a friend, partner or family, or whomsoever it may be, we just need to go and say sorry. This we must do. If you are very embarrassed for your deed, promise with sincerity that next time, something like that will not happen. You must try your best to make them believe that you are really and truly embarrassed and that you are sincerely apologizing. Because more than this, you can do nothing. It could be that you admitting your mistake and saying sorry might make that person feel nice.

Learn from it: Having said sorry, the mistake made cannot be reversed. The act of saying sorry cannot take effect until and unless it is manifested in your actions. Words mean nothing when actions contradict. Try making those changes in your behaviour to avoid similar situations. So that you do not repeat the mistakes in the future and get trapped in your guilt. Reason, if you keep repeating something, then it is not called a mistake but is known as habit. Consider what you can do differently today, and start making those positive changes. So that you do not make those mistakes again. Work on how you can become a better parent, a better spouse, a better friend, a better sibling or just a better human.

I know it's not easy to forgive yourself, but you never know what opportunities you might miss if you keep carrying your past baggage. To conclude, I would just like to say that nobody's perfect. We all screw up and make mistakes, everyone has their bad days and bad memories but then, aren't we all human beings?

Just because we have made some mistake, it does not mean that we need to pay for it for the rest of our lives. Sometimes even good people make wrong choices, but that does not label them as bad for the rest of their lives. It simply means that we all have flaws. So it's okay if you've done something wrong in your past because there is nothing wrong in being wrong once in a while. However, it is totally not okay if you refuse to accept your mistake and keep repeating it again and again.

None is free of faults and wrongs
It's bound to happen in life;
To admit and say 'sorry'
Helps avoid much pain and strife.

43

It's Okay to Ask

Our world today has become such that there is a maddening rush to become independent, in the sense that everyone wants to do everything by themselves. Seeking help from someone for anything seems like asking for a big favour. And even if it does not feel like one, a sense of embarrassment stems from the fact about whether the other person will understand our words, the situation we are in, or the question we have. It would perhaps cause us embarrassment, thinking should the one we are asking for help wonder in their mind that:

Can you not even do this bit?
Can you not understand this?
For once can't you do this bit by yourself?
Do you always need help from others?

Only because we do not wish this to happen we keep to ourselves: our situation, our question and our opinions.

And this hesitation we experience in our work, our personality or relationships spoil them all. Today, I would like to tell everyone, that 'IT IS OKAY TO ASK'. Ask for help, ask a question, ask about a confusion you are having regarding your relationship, work or any other situation. It is totally okay to ask. Also, there is no need for you to do everything by yourself. If you find that you are going the wrong path, don't you seek help? Then you either switch on your Google map or ask for help from a stranger? If that be so, why can't you do the same thing in life?

At times in our life we face certain situations where we do not know or understand what we are supposed to do and we are confused between various options. Rather than struggling with ourself in such situations, it is far better to ask someone responsible. Whatever be the situation, if you do not know about something, asking someone more knowledgeable than yourself makes greater sense. There is little need for that drama—that we know everything and we can do anything. There is not a single person who can claim to know everything in life. Therefore, if in your embarrassment or shame you do not ask a relevant question, you will remain ignorant about the answer all your life. Who suffers the loss? You do. So it is better to ask something you don't know.

Sometimes it may so happen that we suffer emotionally, physically or mentally, and in such situations, we feel weird and even strange to ask for help from anyone. We feel we may become small if we do so and also imagine that the person we are asking may consider us weak, and this makes us think a lot. However, you need to understand that discussing your vulnerable side is not a sign of weakness; it is a sign of your strength, which in essence makes you stronger, wiser and more powerful. Therefore, to have some courage in this regard will benefit us considerably. And only those who call this act a sign of weakness are those who have little or perhaps no courage in their own selves to speak the truth about taking help and assistance from others at the time of their need. And if you possess this quality of asking for help when you require it, then you must be proud of this.

It may also happen in our relationships when instead of asking our near and dear ones directly about a matter which concerns us, we create a pretence in our own mind. This we do assuming that they have thought or planned in a negative manner. Remember, this is nothing but mere hallucination, for the person across has no role in it. And in these kinds of imaginary situations, it is your relationship that gets spoilt. Is it not better that we ask about it and clarify it on the spot? For you never know that they too like you may have created a weird scenario in their mind about the whole thing. Which results in none of you being able to sort out the issue at hand. So it's better to talk, communicate and ask questions, so that there arises no confusion between you and the person across. Not doing this may cause a distance with that person which you may never be able to bridge. So it's okay to ask but not okay to conjure a situation in the mind and arrive at false conclusions, which may cause us pain, trauma, misunderstandings and strained relationships.

To ask a question or not
Is a dilemma we face;
Should we wish to know the truth?
We must inquire with grace.

44

It's Okay to Stress About the Future

Today, most of us are trying to make our future better. Uncounted numbers are busy studying, others are working hard and some youngsters are striving hard at their start-ups. Quite a few are found struggling with their artistic passion and then there are others who are trying to invest their savings into a plausible investment so that their future is safe and secure. By sacrificing our present desires, we feel we will be able to make our future better. But I have a question for everyone who thinks like this. The tomorrow you are so worked up about, are you dead sure that you will see that tomorrow? The dreams you are weaving for tomorrow, are you sure that you will live to see that become a reality? We all know the answer is in the negative.

We do not even know where we will be the next moment. And we also do not know whether we will be there at all or not. Yet, we put Herculean efforts today to make our tomorrow beautiful. I am by no means telling you, you do not keep working for the future and do not think about it. I know, 'this live-in-the-moment' thought we often have cannot make us stop working for our future or thinking about it. We cannot stop trying to make our future secure. But let us not be so caught up in the hurry-scurry of such thoughts, that in the midst of it all, we end up losing our present.

Reason being, what you have today, you will be longing for tomorrow: your age, good health, unbounded zest, you may not have them tomorrow. With age, these things will also lessen or get weaker. So what you can utilize better today, it makes poor sense to leave it for tomorrow. And it often happens that our inability to see our present in the correct perspective becomes the reason for our concern. We have much in our lives, but the thought of what we need tomorrow does not allow us to see and appreciate our present. There's nothing wrong in seeking the best things for yourself: a big house, a huge salary, also a swanky car. Yet, remember all that you possess today, the comfort, peace and contentment which laces your life, to keep that in abeyance or ignoring it would be most inappropriate. Such things add up to a lot by themselves.

What you have today may be someone's dream. That someone may be looking at you from a distance and thinking that whatever he or she has, if I too could achieve that, it would be enough. And despite us having it all, we do not care to value them. Given this thinking, no matter what we attain in our lives, we shall always remain unhappy. Even if we get something really good in our lives, our desire for something better will overshadow it and our present achievements will appear meaningless. For quite a few among us, if they sit quietly and take stock of what they have today, it will be evident that this is what they had once dreamt of. And they have it all in their lives today. And now that they have got it, their dreams have become larger and all that they have has no value whatsoever. Why does this always happen, when we are not able to get something we really want—we value it; and then again after we lose it—we value it; otherwise we don't.

So it's totally okay to work for your future, to have bigger dreams and goals for your future, but it is not at all okay to ignore your present blessings because of that. What you have today is much more precious than what you wish for in the near future. Because, when you want something, there is no guarantee if you will get it or not, but in that rigmarole, whatever you may have should not escape your grasp due to your own foolhardiness. So as long as you have it, value it—be it your situation, your loved ones or your possessions; always be grateful for what you have because not everybody has that.

Future is a bag of dreams
Present—is a gift they say;
Value what life has bestowed
Live it to the brim today.

45

It's Okay If You Miss Someone

It often happens in life that whatever we think and imagine for ourselves may not happen. It may relate to our work, our future planning, deep desires or maybe our relationships. Among these what causes us the maximum pain is our relationships. We make or get into relationships thinking they would stay with us lifelong, but destiny may design otherwise. And the relationship does not continue for a prolonged period. The dreams we had dreamt about that relationship, or the person remain incomplete, for midway our bonding breaks.

At times it happens that a very close or romantic relationship collapses, with which are woven some of the most beautiful memories of our life. This pains us the most and forgetting or erasing such memories causes us much strain and stress. We are constantly reminded about them—but then all that is quite natural. For the ones with whom we have spent precious moments cannot be easily forgotten. The problems ensue when being reminded about them we experience a desire to get back into those broken relationships. This is not a good idea to begin with because you need to understand that you are not being reminded about that person, rather you miss the wonderful times you have had in their company. Such memories compel you to think, maybe getting back in that relationship would help bring back those lost moments. This is not right or correct in many cases. Some relationships end because they were not turning out to be right in the first place, as there were elements in them which were neither right for your future or for your personal growth. But our minds suffer from a strange psychosis; the mind keeps reminding us about that which was nice and wonderful. Therefore, it is not uncommon a happening—to move on takes one a lot of time. Because we keep reminding ourselves of the good times we have spent together and find it impossible to resist them.

If something like this is happening in your life, you need to do two things. The first step being to understand that being reminded of the past and good moments is normal and natural. By itself it is not wrong or unjustified. If you've been with someone you have loved and spent memorable moments with, remembering them is human nature. We are not robots that we press a button and all memories erase. Emotions cannot be switched off or on; they can only be felt. And if you concentrate on your emotions well, you will not just be able to understand them but also find plausible solutions to them. Suppressing them will not push them away but will result in theirs coming back to you with renewed force and vigour.

So it's okay if you are remembering or missing someone, and you feel like crying about it. I suggest remember those moments as much as you want, for there's nothing wrong about it. And neither feeling like this would make you weak. I honestly feel that it will help make you stronger in future.

The next step being that having managed to remember them, you experience a concocted feeling that you want that person back into your life. You may even get a feeling that you have made a mistake by ending that relationship. Right at that moment you need to remind yourself of the reasons why you ended that relationship. Think carefully about the reasons, also about the related issues. And the time you had spent sorting them out. Before ending that relationship, had you not tried your best to set it right? And if your answer is, 'Yes, I tried. I gave it my 100 per cent and seeing many wrongs I was compelled to take that decision,' then it is important to remind yourself about that decision. Because it so happens that often while reminiscing, we tend to think about all that was good but forget those underlying reasons that compelled us to end the relationship. We forget the disrespect we suffered, the disrespect that scarred our self-dignity. It is so important that we remind ourselves about those things, so that, while indulging in good memories, we do not end up taking wrong decisions.

So it's okay if you miss someone who was very close to you. With whom you had spent beautiful moments and made wonderful memories, but it's not okay if in the midst of such remembrances, you forget the lessons you had learnt from it, all which you painfully gathered while ending that relationship. So when you miss the good memories, never forget the disrespect, manipulation, insult, lies, pain and tears.

All bondings aren't meant to stay
Let them go when they have to;
Better ones will take their place
Be sure life will grant your due.

46

It's Okay If You've Had a Bad Past

Once a professor was conducting a class and all the students were keenly listening to him. They were also asking questions and sought clarifications as and when they desired, and the professor was patiently answering them. Somewhere in the class sat a boy who was very quiet and even looked sad. The professor had noticed this boy from the very first day itself but thought it better not to say anything. When even after a few days the boy's behaviour did not change, the professor, keen to know the reason, called the student to his cabin. He asked the boy, 'I have noticed that you remain very silent in class. You even appear sad and do not talk to any of your classmates. Besides, neither do you concentrate on the lecture, nor do you do your homework. Can I help you with some problem that you are experiencing? You can tell me, and I shall try to sort it out.' Haltingly the boy replied, 'Sir, there's something about my past which refuses to let me feel nice. It makes me feel as if I can never go back to being normal in my life, it is becoming very difficult and I am unable to understand what to do.'

The professor was a kind man, and he felt that he would need time with the boy's issues. Deciding it would be a better way to address the issue, he asked the student to come over to his house for dinner that evening.

When the boy reached the professor's house, for a while they spoke about casual things, which made the boy feel at ease. Later, they ate dinner together. After having finished their meal, the professor went into the kitchen to make some lemonade. Knowingly, he put more salt in the drink. Getting back to the living room, he handed over the glass to the boy and said, 'Take this. I have prepared it for you.' Having taken a sip, the boy found it too salty and made a face wincing at the taste. Seeing the boy's reaction, the professor inquired, 'What happened, did you not like the lemonade?' The boy politely replied, 'Nothing like that, sir, it's just that it tastes very salty.'

Expressing surprise, the professor said, 'Oh, I am so sorry! I guess this is not drinkable. Give me the glass, I will put it in the sink.' The boy responded, 'No, sir, it's absolutely alright. If you can mix some water and sugar to it, it would taste just fine. You don't need to throw it all.' The professor said with a smile, 'There, you're absolutely right.' Now this is something you also need to understand about life too. This lemonade is your life, in it the excess salt is the memory of your past. Like you cannot take the salt out of this lemonade, you cannot remove the poor experiences of your past. Those poor experiences have become an integral part of your life. And quite like you said, we can mix some water and sugar in the drink and change its taste; that is exactly what we need to do. We can change the taste of our bad experiences with some sweetness of our good experiences. 'Young man, I wish you to understand this and search for some sweetness in your life.'

For each of us, there is a strong possibility that something like this has happened, which stops us from progressing. Could it be our failed relationships, which does not allow us to trust another one? Again, it can be some personal loss, wherefrom we could never come out. Possibly some failure on the professional front has completely ruined our confidence. Maybe it was some extreme trauma that has drained away the happiness from our lives. However, we must ardently endeavour to bring back the happiness and joy into our lives, not for anyone or the world, but for our own selves. A few bad or poor episodes cannot define your life, but this can only happen when we understand this, and we try to dilute our old bitterness with some sweetness today.

We cannot change whatever has already happened, but how much longer can we keep lugging that weight around? That way we will forever feel heavy in the heart. Old feeling, old experiences coupled with that old failures remain, but unless you make space by erasing them, how on earth would you give space to the new and good ones? Otherwise good moments, good experiences and good opportunities, and special moments would pass you by, but you will never be able to grasp these, as there is no space in your heart and mind to accommodate them. You are already too preoccupied with the negative baggage of your past.

Do you want such A LIFE FOR YOURSELF? Where happiness is in front of you, but you can neither experience nor feel it. If that be so, remember you need to make space for it. I know doing this is far tougher than talking about it, but it is not impossible. No harm in trying and I know when reading this chapter, you would reminisce that you had tried this earlier.

Maybe you're reading this chapter for the same cause—why don't you try it just one more time? Try removing that past baggage and you will realize that the world isn't such a bad place after all. You have the right to be happy once more. You just need to try one more time. So it's okay if you've had a bad past, but that does not mean that you cannot create a better present or a nicer future.

Life is like a lemonade
At times it's salty to taste;
Add sugar and make it good
The drink won't go to a waste.

47

It's Okay to Fall in Love

Where there is love, there is life.

—Mahatma Gandhi

The last chapter of this book also happens to be the most trying and difficult one for me to address and write; despite this fact, it happens to be the closest to my heart. Reason being, I am about to write about such a feeling which is the most important and prime emotion of everyone who's alive and also the most complicated. And that feeling is 'LOVE'. We keep saying we love so and so, we feel such about a person and things like that, but if we sit quietly by ourselves and mull over 'what exactly is love?', then there may only be a very few who would be able to define it correctly. So let us now try to understand this emotion, bear with me because this last chapter also happens to the longest in this book.

'What is love?'

Honestly, love is just a word, until you find someone who gives it a definition. Love is not a course you complete and then you pass an exam, after completing which your relationship moves forward. It is a 'feeling' and it is something which only one understands, who feels it or is going through it. Your definition of love is defined by you yourself and you also define it along with that person with whom you are experiencing it. And it is not necessary that such a feeling is understood by others or for that matter anyone else, but then that's okay. If the relationship of love is yours, then understanding it should also be your arena. This world has turned so mechanical that even when it comes to the deepest of emotions, it tries to experience it along with rules and regulations. But love is not like that, it simply happens. And when we happen to fall in love, we even end up doing such things which once when we saw others doing felt we would never do it in our lives. But at the end, you find such a person that all your 'no's' turn into 'yeses'. When being with such a person, you discover your own definition of love. And that is what one calls love. Where there is just the two of you and no third person. No thoughts of anyone else, no definition of anybody else, no consent of anyone and no space at all to accommodate anyone in it. It's only a tiny little world for the two of you. But once in a while, people go through some confusion with this emotion. Firstly, whatever they are experiencing, is that love in the first place or not? Secondly, is it just a passing infatuation? Thirdly, is it just some kind of dependency? Or perhaps some attachment or habit? There ought to be some basics that would help us define that whatever we are experiencing with a person is nothing else but love. So let us understand a few basics, which must necessarily be present in a relationship so that it may qualify as love.

'Love is friendship'

I guess you all must have seen that movie *Kuch Kuch Hota Hai*. In it I adore a dialogue, '*Pyar dosti hai. Agar woh meri sabse acchi dost nahi ban sakti toh mein usse pyaar nahi kar sakta*.' (Love is friendship. If she cannot become my best friend, then how can I fall in love with her?) I am quite taken in by this dialogue because according to me, love is not just about romance, candle-light dinners, butterflies in the tummy and physical intimacy, it is also a very strong friendship. And friendship is such a relationship where there is no fear about showing our true or real self. We know that our friends would not judge us. We are also not continuously burdened with the baggage of impressing them. We can easily and without any contemplation put forth our inner feelings before them. If you really want to see the real face of someone, I would suggest try to see him or her with his/her good friends. The way or manner in which he or she behaves and acts in front of them is in truth what they exactly are like as a person. Because somewhere or the other, our friends are also our mirrors. And where else can we get a purer relationship than this, where before saying something there is no fear in the mind, neither are there any nervous thoughts? And sharing such a pure bond with our partners is a matter of great luck and fortune.

You must remember something, the first few years of a relationship are taken care of by your hormones, but this does not go on for a long period. However, if you are one another's very good friend, then this relationship would never end. Then the love you both share would always keep increasing. And if you have such a relationship and such a partner, you ensure that you keep him/her very close and with great care. Because this is God's most beautiful gift to you.

'Love is organic'

You must have heard that to keep a relationship going for long, you need to put in arduous effort and a lot of time besides creating special moments so that the relationship moves forward. This is partly right. But if it takes you a lot of effort to put in this kind of effort, and if you feel doing it is like some gigantic task and that you are doing it so that the relationship stays peaceful, then perhaps you do not love that person. Sometimes we are with a person because we are so used to that person that moving out of that relationship becomes not only a big task but also very difficult. Which explains the reason why your putting in that effort seems like quite a task. However, if you really love a person, then the effort is organic: in this case, you just do not find time with them because you need to keep the relationship alive and going but also because you enjoy and like spending time with him or her. You get a lot of happiness and joy. The day-long tiredness you experience gets mitigated when you spend time in their company. While you may not be able to share a meal with the one you love, even a cup of coffee in their company can give you immense peace and contentment. You do not do such things because you deem it a duty as a partner but do it because you want to do it from your heart. Putting in efforts for your loved one feels like an effortless exercise. The reason being, love is not when you are doing good things for the sake of doing it but because you actually enjoy doing it. You enjoy talking to them. You enjoy spending quality time with them. You enjoy exploring new things with them. You enjoy making new memories with them. You just enjoy being with them!

'Love is respect'

You know that in every relationship, there are differences between the partners. Little fights and arguments are natural in all relationships. There can be differences in matters of opinion and choices. Again, there may be material differences that become the root cause of the arguments and fights between the two people involved. And sometimes these little fights and arguments become the very cause that breaks down relationships. So are those relationships good, where they are no fights and differences? Absolutely not. If you keep your authentic self in front of someone, there are bound to be differences in opinion, thoughts and feelings. And during such times, your love will take a back seat. There might also be a phase in your life when you somehow cannot tolerate the person you love. You don't even feel like talking to that person and wish not to see that person's face, for it makes you angry. So what is it that we share and that which keeps us together during such turbulent times? It is sheer respect for our partners. Love can for some times 'vanish', but if you have respect for one another, then the love is certain to return. Because it is certain that sometimes our thought processes will not match, our opinions may not tally, but during such moments, respecting the other person's opinions and thoughts is what we call love. It might also be that we at times might feel that we are right, but at that very moment telling the other person that I do not mean that you are wrong, but that you are very different from me, I respect that fact. There is little need to prove that you are right, and the other person is wrong. We can stick to our point and yet respect the person across. And the true measure of your love is when the two of you have fights and differences. Because only at such times would it be evident how much you respect one another. The reason being that a person who in an adverse situation cannot respect you, such a person will never be able to love you.

'Love is intimacy'

We also know how important physical intimacy is for a relationship. But is intimacy all about having sex? No. It is also about understanding the manner in which your partner enjoys intimacy. It is also about knowing their love language. It is about knowing the ways through which your partner feels love and not just lust. It is about knowing your partner's needs. It is not just about fulfilling your own desires and fantasies but also about understanding and fulfilling the desires your partner has. It is not just about connecting physically but actually feeling the soul connection while you are intimate. You can really feel a soulful connection with your partner while being intimate, but it can happen only when you really and truly love that person. Because it is not just about satisfying the urges of your hormones, but rather about knowing that it is the closest and most raw form of love you can experience with your partner. Sexual intimacy can be the most beautiful thing if there is mutual understanding, love and communication. It happens when you are in complete sync with your partner physically, emotionally and spiritually. And if that happens, intimacy can be very sacred and an experience which is not describable in words. If you can understand this properly, you can really strengthen your bond with your partner and your relationship will never lose its spark.

'Love is commitment'

When you love a person, you really don't want to lose that person. Just the thought of losing the person makes you go through a strange kind of fear, even when you are annoyed with that person, you wish to stay with them. Because love is not always, smooth, cuddly, happy and mushy-gushy. Reason being, you will have your share of arguments, misunderstandings and tensions. You are even going to wake up some mornings and wonder why your partner is still near you! And that's totally normal. And maybe after some time you may feel that it is impossible that you could love another so much. Whatever be the emotion, you would still choose that person at any cost. You can be happy or sad, or angry or celebrating, even tensed or dancing with joy, no matter what the emotion or situation is, you want to share it with that person, who means the world to you. A person, who, no matter what goes on in life, you would always choose—and that is the kind of commitment love requires. So it is important to find the person who deserves such kind of commitment. And if you find that person, no matter how good or bad the day is, choose them always.

As I write this chapter, I feel I may just not stop. I have mostly shared those basics, which I feel your love must have. Beyond this and in addition, you might even have your own definition of love life; you may have your desires and choices and that is how you create your own definition of love. According to me, these five elements help strengthen the bonds of your love life. And if these elements are present in your relationship, then no matter how many ups and downs you may face, you are likely to find a solution to them all. Because that is what a strong love life actually is. And I can surely say that it is the most beautiful feeling in the world.

So it's okay to fall in love, and if it is real love, then everything is not merely okay, but everything is bright and beautiful. Love makes everything look beautiful. Love makes this journey of life beautiful. Hope you find your beautiful. And if you already have found your beautiful then keep your treasure safe from the world, which is gradually maligning the beautiful essence of love.

Love is a beautiful thing
It's rare that you find true love;
If it's found, keep it in heart
It's a gift from God above.

We all wish things are okay in life
If not, then perhaps it's not the end;
Remember, the best is yet to be
Keep some faith and walk around the bend.

'Wishing you health, peace, happiness and prosperity always!'

Warm wishes,
Jaya Kishori

Acknowledgements

This work has been a long and enriching journey. In its entirety, it has been a learning affair that has been both satisfying and a blessing in disguise. Every moment I have spent doing this exercise has been priceless in terms of the experience gained from it and I have felt an overwhelming sense of satisfaction witnessing my lifelong learnings being spelt out in words and on paper.

I have always believed that knowledge and lived experiences must be shared. It is something that has enabled humankind and civilization to move forward. This very idea has helped fuel my imagination and resulted in this work.

To begin with, my deepest reverences to countless sacred Hindu texts and spiritual scriptures—they being the bedrock of my learnings till date. Shri Krishna, the divine lord, whose blessings I have felt every day and, which in turn, have shown me every inch of the way forward on this exciting journey.

A book of this kind and measure can never be completed by any single person. Therefore, I need to thank quite a number of persons to whom I shall always be indebted for this literary creation.

I begin with my parents, who have not just been most supportive and understanding of my endeavours but have showered me with boundless affection. My father, Shiv Shankar Sharma, has been a pillar of strength and motivation. My mother, Sonia Sharma, has helped me imbibe both patience and a refined sense of culture. These qualities have been both instrumental and catalytic in making me what I am today.

My sister Chetna has played a cameo, cheering me up when I needed it the most. Moreover, her artistic talents and immense creativity have also been catalytic and so rejuvenating, giving me newer and fresher ideas to improve.

Thank you to Penguin Random House India and their team, comprising Deepthi Talwar, Manali Das, Vaishali Mathur and Aparajita Pant, for having great confidence and faith in my abilities as a writer and for also being most encouraging and understanding all the while I took to complete this work. I would also like to thank Aakriti Khurana for the cover as well as the sales and marketing team. Getting to publish my first work under the aegis of Penguin Random House India, one of the foremost publication houses of this country and the world, is a matter of great prestige, and I am completely humbled by it. I am grateful for the respect shown by them to me in my maiden venture as a writer. I humbly thank all in the Penguin Random House India team for their unwavering and priceless support and for bestowing upon me this honour.

Amar Agarwala, who has been a teacher and mentor to me, for his guidance and motivation all along. It has kept me focused upon the work even through trying times.

Arpan Mitra, for assisting with this work with his painstaking and meticulous editing.

CA Arun Ji Patodia and his team at BAS and Company, for their continuous guidance, support and assistance as and when I needed it.

I would also like to thank all those who ardently listen to my sessions and discourses and follow me with great dedication through my journey as a spiritual/motivational speaker. It is because of their love and unwavering support that I keep challenging myself to explore new fields of creativity. Every one of them has been my motivation—motivation to do better each and every day.

There are many others whose names are not mentioned here, but I verily thank them all from the bottom of my heart. In all, it has been a marvellous group effort, all of which has made it so much easier for me to complete this treatise. I would like to end by thanking my entire team who have been most supportive and helpful in making this project possible.

Scan QR code to access the
Penguin Random House India website